Living C[...]
J. Dwight Stin[...]

Living
Church

Available now...
Learning Mission, Living Mission
Churches That Work
Glynis LaBarre

Empowering Laity, Engaging Leaders
Tapping the Root for Ministry
Susan E. Gillies and M. Ingrid Dvirnak

Caring Pastors, Caring People
Equipping Your Church for Pastoral Care
Marvin A. McMickle

Making Friends, Making Disciples
Growing Your Church through Authentic Relationships
Lee B. Spitzer

www.judsonpress.com / 800-4-JUDSON

Learning Mission, Living Mission

Churches That Work

GLYNIS LaBARRE

J. DWIGHT STINNETT, SERIES EDITOR

Living Church

JUDSON PRESS
PUBLISHERS SINCE 1824

Join our mailing list for updates and special offers.
www.judsonpress.com/mailing_list.cfm

Learning Mission, Living Mission: Churches That Work
© 2012 by Judson Press, Valley Forge, PA 19482-0851
All rights reserved.

Judson Press has made every effort to trace the ownership of all quotes. In the event of a question arising from the use of a quote, we regret any error made and will be pleased to make the necessary correction in future printings and editions of this book.

Unless otherwise noted, Bible quotations marked NIV are from the HOLY BIBLE, NEW INTERNATIONAL VERSION®. NIV®. Copyright © 1973, 1978, 1984, 2011 by Biblica, Inc.™ Used by permission. All rights reserved worldwide.

Interior design by Wendy Ronga at Hampton Design Group. Cover design by Tobias Becker and Birdbox Graphic Design. www.birdboxdesign.com.

Library of Congress Cataloging-in-Publication
LaBarre, Glynis.
Learning mission, living mission: churches that work/Glynis LaBarre.—1st ed.
p. cm. Includes bibliographical references and index. ISBN 978-0-8170-1725-5
(pbk.: alk. paper) 1. Mission of the church. 2. Church. I. Title.
BV601.8.L26 2012
266—dc23

Printed in the U.S.A.
First Edition, 2012.

Contents

Foreword

The people of God have always been a risk-taking, creative people. Across their history they have been willing to imagine what it means to be God's people on the journey in strange new lands. Ours is, again, one of those "strange" places where God's Spirit is upsetting settled assumptions about being church and where we are called to be Christ's witnesses in very disruptive times.

Congregations today find themselves confronted with challenges to mission and ministry they could not have imagined even a decade ago. Whenever these disruptions occur, all kinds of "gurus" come along with "expert" solutions to "fix" the church. They come from corporate America or from nonprofit organizations. They come from national consulting firms or heavily endowed foundations. And most folk in our congregations and many of our local church leaders know the solutions of these imported gurus really don't work.

What we need are people who know us. We need wise guides who have lived in our house and walked in our shoes, so to speak. We need perceptive readers of our stories who know the language and feel the issues; they are "our" people who have loved, lived, wept, and shouted for joy among us. This is what you have in this book.

As a former local church pastor and church transformation strategist for her own national denomination, Glynis LaBarre isn't one of those master chefs who barges into your kitchen with a prepackaged add-water-and-stir recipe. She does not pretend to offer a simplistic formula or a one-size-fits-all program for transformation and renewal. Instead, she has written for you a practical guide for engaging the communities and neighborhoods where you live with the gospel message. It is, she explains, a kind of experiment in missional ministry.

To begin, she presents some basic convictions about what God is up to in our time. She then goes on to walk you through key steps in implementing strategic missional change in your congregation. She doesn't position herself as a know-all expert as much as a fellow storyteller, one who encourages you to explore your own community and write your own missional story. As a wonderfully reflective and caring member of the Christian church family, she invites you onto this strange, risk-taking missional journey.

What I particularly like about what Glynis is doing is that she gives you the tools to shape a mission engagement that is *yours*, that comes out of your people and their lives. Her Missional Church Learning Experience model starts not with some plan to make you into the cookie-cutter replica of someone else's success story. Rather, it begins with where *you* are and makes it possible for your church to become the best version of itself, for the benefit of your congregation and of your community. The MCLE experiment is built on the conviction that the Spirit is really active in your local church, and in the midst of your stories God has already conceived amazing ways of being a gospel witness in your community.

Dr. Alan J. Roxburgh
Director, The Missional Network

Preface to the Series

"What happened? Just a few years ago we were a strong church. We had thriving ministries and supported a worldwide mission effort. Our community knew us and cared about what we did. Now we're not sure if we can survive another year."

It is a painful conversation I have had with more church leaders than I can name here.

In each conversation, I explain how images such as *meltdown*, *tsunami*, *earthquake*, and *storm* have been used to describe the crisis developing in the North American church over the last twenty-five years. The American Religious Identification Survey 2008 underscored our present crisis by showing that not just one local congregation, but nearly every church is being swamped by the changes.

Volumes have already been written in analysis of the current situation and in critique of the church. To the questioning church leader I suggest a few books and workshops that I know, trying to avoid the highly technical works. But all the analysis overwhelms the church leader. "Yes, I am sure that is true. But what do we do? When I look at what is happening and I hear all the criticism, I wonder if the church has a future at all. Do we deserve one?"

I emphasize that there are no simple answers and that those who offer simplistic solutions are either deceived or deceiving. There is no "church cookbook" for today (and I'm not sure there ever really was one). I try to avoid an equally simplistic, pietistic answer.

Still, the church leader presses. "So is the church dead? Do we just need to schedule a funeral and get over it? We are all so tired and frustrated."

I do not accept the sentiment of futility and despair about the future of the church. I believe the church is alive and persists not because of what we do, but because of what God has done and continues to do in the church.

The pain is real, however, as are the struggle and the longing. I want to help church leaders such as this one understand, but not be overwhelmed by, the peculiar set of forces impacting the church today. But information is not enough. I want to encourage them with specific things that can be done, without implying that success is guaranteed or that human effort is sufficient. I want them to learn from what others are doing, not to copy them mechanically, but to use what others are doing as eyeglasses to look closely at their own context. I want them to avoid all the churchy labels that are out there and be a living church in their community, empowered and sustained by the living God.

Those of us who work with groups of churches and who pay attention to the things that are happening around us know that several forces are having a devastating effect on the church today. Both formal studies and personal observation identify at least eight key areas where the impact has been especially acute.

These areas are shrinking numbers, brokenness in and around us, declining leadership base, narrowing inward focus, biblical illiteracy, financial pressures, overwhelming diversity, and unraveling of spiritual community. It is not hard to see how each of these is related to the others.

Living Church is a series from Judson Press intended to address each of these forces from a congregational perspective. While our authors are well-informed biblically, theologically, and topically, these volumes are not intended to be an exercise in ecclesiastical academics. Our intent is to empower congregational leaders (both clergy and laity) to rise to the challenge before us.

Our goal is not merely to lament our state of crisis, but to identify creative and constructive strategies for our time and place so that we can move on to effective responses. Our time and place is the American church in the twenty-first century.

The first volume in this series, *Making Friends, Making Disciples*, by Dr. Lee Spitzer, addresses the issue of shrinking numbers by reminding us of the spiritual discipline of being and making friends—not with some ulterior motive, but because God has called us to relationship.

The second volume, *Caring Pastors, Caring People*, by Dr. Marvin McMickle, confronts the growing brokenness within and around the church by challenging pastors and laity to provide pastoral care first within the congregation, and then to the community beyond the church.

In the third volume, *Empowering Laity, Engaging Leaders*, Susan Gillies and Ingrid Dvirnak consider the declining leadership base in many churches today and assert, "Church vitality depends on the involvement of both clergy and laity in meaningful ministry."

This fourth volume, *Learning Mission, Living Mission* by Glynis LaBarre addresses the growing (and troubling) response that many churches have in this time of crisis: an inward focus that reflects a survival mentality. Since the 1970s, under the creative influence of Lesslie Newbigen, the church has developed an emerging understanding of "mission" as something that happens not only across the sea but also across the street. Today, the language of the "missional church" is everywhere, and at the same time it seems to defy definition. However, this volume highlights two key insights at the heart of transforming an increasingly self-centered church. First, mission is God's, and the church is invited (expected!) to participate in it. Second, mission demands the church look outside its four walls.

While informed by and using the language of "missional church," LaBarre focuses on a particular aspect of this concern (the immediate community of the church) and a particular model for engaging the church in community mission (the Missional Church

Learning Experience). Learning by experience is central to this model, which reintroduces the local congregation to the heart of God's mission. Mission is more than sending dollars to support professional missionaries in faraway exotic places. At its core, mission is about announcing, demonstrating, and promoting the Reign of God—beginning with the highways, alleys, neighborhoods, and office buildings that surround the church.

Fundamentally, this call to "learn mission" is an invitation for churches "to travel together . . . learning from each other . . . in a hands-on process." Glynis describes four simple steps for a church to start looking outward: Team-build, Listen, Look, Discern. This is a practical strategy for congregations to lose their blinders, look outside, and be the community of mission that God has called every church to be.

Rev. Dr. J. Dwight Stinnett
Series Editor
Executive Minister
American Baptist Churches, Great Rivers Region

Acknowledgments

When we read in Revelation 21–22 of the vision for the new heaven and the new earth, it is striking that it describes a city. A city requires many interactive, interdependent relationships. For me, writing the Missional Church Learning Experience (MCLE) story has been an experience in Christian community. It could not have happened without the sacrificial involvement of many people whose names do not appear on the cover of the book, but to whom I want to express my gratitude:

Charles Scalise, Professor of Church History at Fuller Theological Seminary in Seattle, for the many hours of careful reading and correcting of the original draft of the book. He asked all the right questions.

Tom Sine, well-known author in the study of functional Christianity, for his gracious hospitality as he assisted my early development in understanding the missional church movement.

Eddie Hammett, ministry coach and noted author, for teaching me the coaching skills used in the MCLE process that continue to add to its effectiveness.

Ron Carlson, professor and colleague in the missional church field, for introducing me to important resources and generously using his teaching talent to inform my many questions about the missional church movement.

Cassandra Williams, beloved friend, colleague, and outstanding Christian educator, for using her excellent editing skills to make the story a much clearer, richer experience for us all.

The Judson Press team for providing the opportunity for the

MCLE story to be told and for patiently walking me through the publication process. I now have a greater appreciation for the behind-the-scenes work involved in publication.

To all the MCLE churches, regional ministers, and staff of the American Baptist Home Mission Societies, you are all heroes in my book for your love, faith, and hard work.

To the King and the Kingdom; may God be honored by our efforts to share the Good News.

What's the Big Idea?

Every story has a beginning, although we rarely recognize it at the time. For this book, the story began on August 1, 2007, with the proverbial "good news, bad news" phone call. The good news was that a charitable trust I had worked with was inviting us to apply for a grant to help small church ministries. The bad news was that they wanted a completely new initiative, different from previous grant efforts, and the deadline was August 10, 2007—giving me just ten days to write an innovative grant. Fortunately, I was already in conversation with previous grant participants about future church ministry, and two of them strongly advocated for an initiative related to the missional church movement.

The growing missional movement shifts the church's focus from inside the church walls to outward concern and involvement with the surrounding community's well-being. The hope is to bring the gospel of Jesus Christ to life in the local community through engagement. While the missional church movement had been receiving a great deal of attention among church leaders and some individual churches were increasing their community interaction by applying missional principles, no simple process for traditional churches to explore the missional movement was available at that time. With only ten days until deadline, I approached my ministry supervisors, Rev. Dr. David Laubach and Rev. Dr. Marilyn Turner, with an idea for a learn-by-doing approach to introduce churches to missional concepts. With their support, I wrote a proposal for the Missional Church Learning Experience (MCLE), which would begin with the formation of seven learning communities, each made up of teams from six to twelve churches. The learning communities would be introduced to missional ideas, and then each church mission team would practice missional principles by designing and implementing a small, interactive community project. Reconvening the learning communities throughout the year would allow for sharing experiences and learning from one another. The intent was that the combination of the learn-by-doing approach with the sharing of experiences would create an inspiring space for experimentation with the missional movement. I managed to meet the deadline for the grant, and the typical rush of fall ministry left me little time to wonder about the outcome.

Several weeks after submitting the grant, I received a call from the grant trustee with questions about using the grant to involve churches in the missional church movement. The trustee explained that the original intent of the grant was to help small churches in small towns with maintenance items like a new roof or replacing a furnace. She was not from a religious background and had no idea what churches did beyond meeting on Sunday morning for worship. Why would churches benefit from being involved with their communities? It was a great opportunity to express my developing missional understanding.

As we talked, I told the trustee how much church life was changing in the United States and that many churches were more in need of fresh vitality in their ministry than a new roof and more in danger of closing than freezing without a new furnace.[1] It was clear from our discussion that this was a stretch in her thinking, but she was interested and cared enough to consider the possible advantages that being missional might bring to churches. Just before Christmas the news came that the grant proposal had been accepted, and that meant January would begin the challenge of inviting others to get involved with this national experiment in the missional church movement.

In January 2008, notification was sent to the regional executive ministers of the American Baptist Churches USA with the "Missional Church Learning Experience Guidelines" (see Appendix A, page 86), inviting them to form an MCLE learning community in partnership with the American Baptist Home Mission Societies. Enough funds were available to form the proposed seven learning communities. I waited expectantly, wondering if anyone would respond. To my joyful surprise, regions began making inquiries almost immediately. Working with each regional executive minister and each region's appointed local coordinator, we reviewed the MCLE guidelines and wrote a learning agreement to ensure that the experience would complement their unique values and accomplish the specific goals of the region.

Much of what has happened through the MCLE is due to the brave experimenters from the sixty-six churches who participated in the original seven learning communities. Their willingness to try an untested process led to many improvements. At the time of this writing, more than thirty learning communities have formed, involving over a thousand church leaders from more than two hundred churches in fifteen states. These leaders represent a broad range of Christian thought, church sizes, community settings, and cultures. Together they share the common purpose, with millions of Christians worldwide, of seeking to understand and follow God's will in this time of great change and great opportunity.

Key Components of the Missional Church Learning Experience

The Key Role of Relationships

For Christians to have a positive impact in a watching world, we must begin with the quality of our relationships, cultivating love, trust, respect, and joy. This starts with the key roles of the MCLE facilitator, the local coordinator, and the learning community. The facilitator will lead others through the process. The coordinator is a person selected by the local group of interested churches to serve as their representative and work with the facilitator in gathering and supporting the group through the process. And the learning community is composed of small teams from each participating church, learning the process on behalf of their church.

The facilitator needs to invest much effort in building good relationships with the local coordinator and the church teams throughout the experience. The first step in forming an MCLE is a review of the guidelines, a roadmap for the experience that includes a request form and learning agreement used by the facilitator and coordinator as a tool for ongoing conversation and improvements throughout the process.

To ensure that the church teams remain the center of the experience, the facilitator uses coaching skills throughout the process. Good coaching involves asking effective questions and leading discussions that help the churches learn from each other's experiences. A coach approach assumes that the churches have the skills and talents necessary to serve God's mission with their communities and that they are willing to develop to become even more effective. Coaching also involves letting the group find their own answers to tough questions, rather than deciding for them what works in their community ministry setting. Another important aspect of the facilitator's role is that of encourager. Thinking in new patterns and trying new skills can be awkward for many people. It is important for the facilitator to have the ability to encourage the church teams in every effort along the way and to work diligently through constant communication to starve discouragement, giving it no neglect to feed upon.

The key role of the coordinator requires several qualities that make this person effective in developing and holding together the group of churches. A coordinator's knowledge of local culture is helpful as she or he begins to offer the MCLE opportunity to local churches. It is also useful if the person selected for this role knows which churches are ready to attempt something new and are not currently involved in internal conflicts that might be detrimental to the health of the learning community. Another crucial quality is attention to detail because the coordinator plans session arrangements and communicates details, factors that affect attendance. This role also requires good follow-up skills. The scattered nature of churches necessitates regular communication and what amounts to "pastoral care" (using a variety of methods such as phone calls and Internet tools) to keep participants engaged in the process between sessions.

Most important, the coordinator needs to provide spiritual leadership throughout the experience, conducting opening worship at MCLE meetings and providing ongoing prayer. The ability to call others to exercise their faith makes a profound difference in the attitudes and achievements that the learning community experiences. Some coordinators may choose to go further in the process by training to become MCLE facilitators to replicate the MCLE process for future learning communities. An MCLE facilitator's guide and training seminar are in development to assist persons who wish to learn more about forming this missional experience for their own church or small groups of local churches. Check the publisher's website for further details, www.judsonpress.com.

The Key Role of Community

The MCLE learning community, which is comprised of mission teams from a minimum of six churches, allows for the interchange of experiences necessary to form a vibrant learning environment. The maximum number of twelve teams is intended to ensure enough time for all to participate. Each mission team is encouraged to have five members, including the church pastor or other appointed leader, three lay leaders, *and one member between 15 and 29 years of age.* The young adult member serves as a cultural guide to each team since that member was born into this time of accelerated change. For young adults, this time of change is their native culture. Mission teams are advised that they will be teaching one another what they learn about being missional as they actually design and implement a small interactive community engagement. Learning takes place as the facilitator guides the churches through the process, leading discussions and asking questions, while the teams share their experiences.

One of the most important lessons from the MCLE is how much more the individual churches learn when they share their experiences with a group of other congregations. Sometimes we are more motivated to help and encourage others than we would be to help and encourage ourselves. Each session of the MCLE includes intentional efforts to bond the church mission teams to one another— through joining together in worship, forming a learning community covenant, praying for one another, and celebrating with dedication ceremonies. The commitment that is developed among local churches during the process is an added bonus, strengthening both the learning community and the areas in which the member churches serve.

The Key Role of Active Learning

The primary premise of the MCLE is that most people do not fully learn until they apply ideas to real-life situations and until the principles they practice become second nature.[2] For that reason, the entire MCLE process is designed around actually *doing* a small project with the community, which the church teams use as their case study in missional values. Missional principles introduced in the first session are repeated throughout the process, but at an increasingly deeper level as each team reflects on their experiences along the way. The teams engage in assignments between sessions that are designed to create healthy repeatable patterns that will assist participants in multiplying future missional efforts if they choose to continue on the missional path. All of the sessions use participative activities to give each church team, and the learning community as a whole, opportunities to add new ideas about application for their church ministries. Each of the three sessions are approximately four months apart, with assignments and technology sessions using conference calls and online video or web conferencing in between to advance the community involvement of geographically distant participants. Training includes understanding rapid change; planning forward; main missional ideas; key steps to becoming missional; multiplying missional efforts; the church's role in being missional; managing change in positive ways; and the importance of sharing our stories.

* * *

These key components—relationships, community, and active learning—create a supportive environment for churches to explore their response to the rapid changes in our culture. The following chapters are arranged in the order of an actual MCLE learning community experience. They offer a taste of the process to introduce individuals and churches to the missional movement, to help churches form missional learning communities in their own locations, and to support MCLE-participating churches in their process. Throughout the book you will read thoughts and comments by past participants to help you learn from their experiences. Traveling with other churches on this road to discovery can be exciting and challenging, but never dull, as we share ourselves with others and learn together. Fasten your seat belt, the future is here!

Key Points
■ The growing missional movement shifts the church's focus from inside the church walls to outward concern and involvement with the surrounding community's well-being.

■ For Christians to have a positive impact in a watching world, we must begin with the quality of our relationships.

■ The young adult member serves as a cultural guide to each team since that member was born into this time of accelerated change.

■ One of the most important lessons from the MCLE is how much more individual churches learn when they share their experiences with a group of other churches.

■ The primary premise of the MCLE is that most people do not fully learn until they apply ideas to real-life situations and until the principles they practice become second nature.

Notes

1. Tom Elrich, "Bad News, Good News," *Morning Walk* (blog), Morning Walk Media, September 16, 2010, www.morningwalk media.com/morning-walk-media-blog/bad-news-good-news.

2. Malcolm S. Knowles, *The Modern Practice of Adult Education: Andragogy versus Pedagogy*, rev. ed. (Englewood Cliffs: Prentice Hall/Cambridge, 1988).

CHAPTER 1

Congratulations — You Have Been Chosen

Congratulations—you have been chosen to serve God during a time of unparalleled change. You are experiencing the most accelerated rate of change in human experience. Famed physicist Dr. Michio Kaku states, "More scientific knowledge has been accumulated just in the last few decades than in all of human history. And by 2100, this scientific knowledge will again double many times over."[1] The University of California at Berkeley has estimated that the world generates in one year 57,000 times the total of all information currently in the Library of Congress. This means that 70 percent of all information in the world today has been created since the introduction of the World Wide Web on August 6, 1991.[2] At the current rate, information is doubling every three years, meaning that we will have 16 times more information by 2015 than we had in 2003.[3] We accept this pace of change as normal because we who are alive today were born into it, and humans are a very adaptive species. However, even as we sense an increase in the rate of change, we fail to measure the intensity of that change and its significance for our own environment.

To help you grasp the explosion of change in just the last fifty years, take a few moments to play the "Change Game." Think back to what the world was like in the late 1950s and early 1960s. If you are too young to remember that time, think about some of the well-known television shows of that period, which you may have seen as reruns, such as *The Andy Griffith Show*, *I Love Lucy*, or *Leave It to Beaver*. What changes have happened in the following areas in the last fifty years?

- Science & Technology
- Sports & Entertainment
- Transportation
- Medicine & Healthcare
- U.S. Culture

Just for fun, compare your list of changes to answers given by people who have played the Change Game across the country (Appendix B, page 101). Did you experience any surprises? What would you add to their list? For some, an activity like this provides the first opportunity to visualize the extent of change in their lifetimes. In his classic 1970 book, *Future Shock*, Alvin Toffler predicts this escalating change and questions humans' ability to successfully adapt to the rapid increase. He describes future shock as "culture shock in one's own society. But its impact is far worse. For the most part travelers have the comforting knowledge that the culture they left behind will be there to return to. The victim of future shock does not."[4] Reading Toffler's book today reveals that he was unable to imagine the far-reaching effects of change that we experience daily in our lives, such as the common use of the Internet or technologies like the smartphone. Understanding change's exponential nature helps to explain the unsettling effects of change on cultures worldwide.

The Impact of Change on the Christian Church in the United States

While rapid change has profoundly affected every aspect of life in the U.S. over the last fifty years, one of the most fundamental societal shifts has come in the role of the church within the culture. Just fifty years ago weekly church attendance was normative, with the substantial majority of Americans regularly participating in a Christian faith community. Today, less than 17.7 percent of Americans attend church regularly, defined as twice a month or more.[5] This dramatic drop in church attendance coincides with an explosion in the U.S. population, from 178 million in 1959 to more than 309 million in 2009.[6] Many churchgoers may not have made the connection between changes in their church's attendance and the bigger picture of change in our country. They may be even less aware that the decline of Christian influence in the culture is likely to continue, because much of the population increase is among people under forty years of age whom neither current churches nor new churches are reaching.

The reduced attendance in the pews does not fully measure the loss of the church's influence in the culture. Sunday morning is no longer recognized as a time set apart for worship. It now competes with a myriad of options. The vast increase in dual-working households has transformed Sunday morning into a time for families to relax, relieving the pressure of their overscheduled lives. Relatedly, Christian ministry has dropped from being one of the

"We were at a point where we were wondering if we could even survive financially when the MCLE was mentioned. We only averaged about thirty in worship. We are up to fifty now. The community involvement helped put a church that had a history of splits in a new light, and we hope that is just one step in healing the church to become one that is serving the Lord faithfully. Now more than 85 percent of our members give their time and talents in community service, and we are also stronger in mission giving, in spite of our size."
—First Baptist Church, Knoxville, IA

most respected professions in the country to being ranked as one of the most stressful occupations and one that is highly detrimental to family.[7] More than half the clergy in the U.S. serve churches that cannot afford to pay a full-time salary,[8] and for many churches, providing health insurance for the pastor and family is impossible.[9]

How is such a dramatic cultural shift possible in one lifetime? Let's take a look at some of the national trends that have affected the church since the 1930s. People who grew up in those years witnessed a dramatic shift from an agrarian society to an unmatched industrial power almost overnight. During World War II the U.S. experienced an unprecedented retooling of industry, from building domestic items like railroads and farm machinery to manufacturing military equipment such as aircraft carriers, tanks, and planes. Americans were also becoming increasingly aware of their role as a world power that is part of a bigger global system. Faith in science and modern methodology increasingly competed with faith in God as the source of hope for the human race.

The post-war baby boom and the growth of urban centers with industrial jobs created another massive change in the country's lifestyle: the development of suburbs. The suburban sprawl of the 1950s and 1960s accelerated the increased use of cars and caused explosive growth in highway systems. The church adapted magnificently to this rapid change by starting tens of thousands of new churches conveniently located near growing suburban families. Churches also developed multitudes of new services including nursery care, youth groups, women's ministries, and summer camping programs. But the changes would not hold still.

The 1960s were tumultuous years. The growing prominence of television widened our perspective from local to national and later global. The Cold War stimulated enormous advances in science, including the continued development of atomic weapons, which brought the world to the edge of nuclear war. Advances in space technology created the first orbiting satellites, leading to further space exploration, which was crowned by the moon landings at the end of the decade and opened the door to vast new technologies. The assassinations of public figures such as President John F. Kennedy, Attorney General Robert Kennedy, and civil rights leader Dr. Martin Luther King Jr. left the country gasping for stability. Large-scale social movements, including Civil Rights and President Johnson's "Great Society," exploded the "separate but equal" myth. The antiestablishment "hippie" culture introduced a sexual revolution that overturned long-held behavioral standards, accented by the introduction of the birth control pill. Young adults began questioning government and military authority during the Vietnam conflict. News of violence, such as the shooting of protesting students at Kent State, erupted around our nation and catapulted onto television screens in homes across the U.S. These serious upheavals caused many young Americans, born in the post–World War II period, to question the faith of their parents and the role of the church in light of vast cultural changes and scientific development.

As the 1970s took hold, the burgeoning women's movement began demanding a broader range of choices and opportunities, which led to shifts in the expectations for both men and women at home and at work. The Supreme Court's decision to legalize abortion in Rowe vs. Wade exposed a growing national schism over the struggle between individual freedom and government control. At

"The MCLE isn't rocket science, but it does provide structure that allows a church to practice some steps and then evaluate the impact on the church as well as the local community. I went back to my leadership group at Rivergate Community Church and told them about the MCLE, and we got excited."
—Rev. Carren Woods, Rivergate Community Church, Portland, OR

the same time, public trust in political leaders was further eroded as Vice President Agnew was forced to resign amidst charges of tax evasion, and the Watergate scandal swallowed Nixon's presidency. The huge economic problems that stalled under the Carter administration forced many families permanently into the two-income model just to survive.

After decades of constant upheaval, the country was seeking stability and found an expression of that in the Evangelical movement that flourished in portions of the country in the 1980s and 1990s. The growing challenge for the church in the U.S. during these decades was how to reach the large percentage of church-raised "Boomers" who had dropped out of the church as young adults. Throughout the late 1970s and 1980s, portions of the church creatively adapted to this challenge by adopting pop culture, music, and technologies that attracted these young adults. Megachurches such as Willow Creek and Saddleback became models for many efforts throughout the country to capture this generation's spiritual energy.

However, every success brings some unintended consequences, and the so-called attractional movement was no exception. Most notably, as the culture continued to slide deeper and deeper into consumerism, the attractional methods used by churches fed the consumer addiction, making church choice a matter of selecting which congregation could best meet one's needs. Churches began offering a broader range of services to attract more people. Worship involved an ever-escalating techno-wow quality with big screens, sound equipment, and professional-quality music performance. All of this activity required a bigger investment of time, money, and energy from the church, drawing on its resources to increase its size just to stay competitive and making its mission more and more internally focused.

The second unintended side effect of the attractional movement was that many small churches felt pushed to the sidelines and unable to compete. In a country where nearly 60 percent of

Christian churches average fewer than 100 members,[10] some small churches became depressed at their lack of growth and gave up trying to attract new members, choosing rather to focus on keeping and caring for their existing members. Others turned their out-of-date condition into a status symbol of their faithfulness to tradition. The overall result of the megachurch trend was that many small churches felt too small, too old, and too poor in resources to have significant impact on their communities, so they dropped out of community life.

Regardless of the effect, the attractional church growth methods of the 1970s are now forty years behind us. These four decades have produced two generations who are now adults and one generation of children. While contemporary worship and church growth techniques worked to bring back some young adults of the Boomer generation, they failed to reach the majority, who went on to form their lives apart from the church. That very large group of young adults raised their children outside the church and the knowledge of the Christian faith. Today aging "Boomers," who are now reaching their sixties, are seeing their adult children of Generation X (born between 1965 and 1982) and the Millennial Generation (born between 1983 and 1999), and their grandchildren and even great

"When I heard the message about accelerating change, I was dismayed to think about my small church closing its doors in the future. I was wrong to come to that conclusion. We have tried connecting with our community and see that we can be a vital part once we get outside our own doors. The MCLE . . . has readjusted our sights so that we show our love for the Lord in ways the community recognizes."

—Laura H. Austin, member of First Baptist Church, Mansfield, CT grandchildren (the "iGeneration"—iPod, iPhone, and iPad—born after 2000), living with no significant knowledge of the Christian faith in a world that is increasingly high-tech and secular.[11] Much of the U.S. is now three generations removed from experiencing the church as the center of faith, with only 13 percent making their decisions based on the principles taught in the Bible.[12] This secular culture is not typically hostile toward God or even toward the Christian faith, but it simply does not consider church attendance to be the only way (or best way) to know God. This shift in perspective also explains why attractional methods are no longer effective in bringing young adults to church; the vast majority of Americans under forty years of age simply do not have enough church background to draw them to either traditional or contemporary worship, and most churches have little else to offer.

Future-Focused Church

As shocking as the transition to an increasingly secular nation may be for Christians who are old enough to remember a different culture, it is nothing compared to the change that is coming in the next twenty years. Change accelerates change. Consider for example that it took the human race more than six thousand years to get from foot transportation to the stage coach, but only one hundred years to get from the locomotive to rocket ships landing on the moon. Just as the World Wide Web has become a part of daily life in just twenty years, so too coming technologies will change the values and systems of today at an ever-increasing rate.

Think for a moment about some of the technologies that are currently on the edge of our existence that will become mainstream in the next twenty years. We have only begun to experiment with lasers for surgery and military weapons. Drone aircraft are flown by people who sit thousands of miles away. Nanotechnology promises to allow particles too small to be seen by the naked eye to clear arteries without surgery. Gene therapy will make it possible to avoid some diseases and illnesses altogether.[13] Stem cells from our own bone marrow are now being used to regrow body parts.[14] *National Geographic* tells of scientists working to revive extinct life forms from DNA.[15] Biology and robotics combine to replace damaged and missing limbs.[16] Smarter and faster computers will demonstrate Artificial Intelligence, which will become a part of our daily lives.[17] All of these developments are actually now possible and are awaiting further use.[18]

This is not science fiction; this is the future upon us. Included in these shifts will be a population increase in the U.S. to more than 438 million by 2050, with 82 percent of the increase coming from immigrants arriving between 2005 and 2050 and their offspring. These demographics move us from being predominantly Euro-American to multicultural.[19] All of these changes will continue to affect the culture and the role of the church in American life.

With rapid change as the new normal, how is the church equipping Christians to have impact with the Good News of Jesus Christ? Most continue with the practices of the 1950s and 1960s, repeating their annual calendar of events with little change. While this tactic may effectively retain a small group of young people raised within these cultural expressions of Christianity, it has little effect on bringing the gospel of Jesus Christ to the increasing number of people who have lived their entire lives outside the church. This "business as usual" approach by churches in effect turns the

"The MCLE encapsulates the model, mandate, and message of Jesus that can be shaped to any church based on its mission, vision, purpose, and legacy, identified by how the faith and love of Jesus Christ is to be lived out in Jerusalem, Judea, and Samaria."
    —Rev. Mary Tellis, former Area Minister, American Baptist Churches of the Rocky Mountains

church's mission into one of maintaining a smaller and smaller sub-culture until Jesus returns.

But other Christians are looking at the changes of the past fifty years and of those ahead and are becoming more future-focused, attempting to learn the skill of planning forward. They understand that, in a time of accelerating change, any effort to adapt to changes that have already happened will leave them further and further behind reality. Rather than expending energy on adapting to changes that have occurred, they are asking the question, "If most Americans will no longer come into the church to hear the Good News of Jesus Christ or practice the faith, how do we take the gospel of Jesus Christ to the people?" From this future-focused thinking, some experimental efforts are springing up to engage the world with the gospel of Jesus Christ—a gospel these Christians believe has the power to set the world right-side up.

It was in this experimental climate that the Missional Church Learning Experience (MCLE) formed. The MCLE invites church-es to travel together for a period of time, learning from each other about the possible future effectiveness of Christianity in America in a practical, hands-on process. This experimental model encourages conversation among church teams about the changes they are experiencing in their own communities. It provides action steps to try new ideas within their communities, and a safe environment to discuss what they learn from getting involved in God's mission out-side the church. The MCLE opens the door to creative exploration and a mind-set that God is opening doors of opportunity for the church in the changes we are all experiencing. The next chapters invite you to "virtually" attend a MCLE learning community and hear for yourself what others have learned through this experience.

Key Points

■ Many churchgoers may not have made the connection between changes in their church's attendance and the bigger picture of change in our country; even as we sense the rate of change increasing, we fail to measure the intensity of that change and its significance for our own environment.

■ The attractional methods used by churches fed the consumer addiction, making church choice a matter of selecting which congregation could best meet one's needs, and leaving many small churches feeling too small, too old, and too poor in resources to have significant impact on their communities.

■ Much of the U.S. is now three generations removed from experiencing the church as the center of faith. The vast majority of Americans younger than forty years of age simply do not have enough church background to draw them to either traditional or contemporary worship, and most churches have little else to offer.

■ As shocking as the transition to an increasingly secular nation may be for Christians who are old enough to remember a different culture, it is nothing compared to the change that is coming in the next twenty years.

■ Future-focused Christians understand that, in a time of accelerating change, any effort to adapt to changes that have already happened will leave them further and further behind reality.

Notes

1. Michio Kaku, *Physics of the Future* (New York: Doubleday, 2011), 6.

2. Thomas L. Friedman, *The World Is Flat* (New York: Picador, 2005), 61.

3. Scott MacGregor, *The Future Foretold*, rev. ed. (Switzerland: Aurora Production, 2008), chapter 10.

4. Alvin Toffler, *Future Shock* (New York: Bantam Books, 1970), 11.

5. Rebecca Barnes and Lindy Lowry, "The American Church in Crisis," *Outreach Magazine*, May/June 2006.

6. U.S. Census Bureau.

7. Richard J. Krejcir, "Statistics on Pastors" from *Francis A. Schaeffer Institute of Church Leadership Development* (2007), www.churchleadership.org/apps/articles/default.asp?articleid=42347&columnid=4545.

8. Bob Smietana, "More preachers need a 'day job,' too," *The Nashville Tennessean*, June 20, 2010.

9. "Many clergy vulnerable to health insurance loss," *The Christian Century*, August 25, 2009.

10. National Congregations Study, www.soc.duke.edu/ natcong, (accessed August 4, 2012).

11. William Strauss and Neil Howe, *Millennials Rising: The Next Generation* (New York: Vintage, 2000), 3–120.

12. Michael Frost, *Exiles: Living Missionally in a Post-Christian Culture* (Peabody, MA: Hendrickson, 2006), 6.

13. Jennifer S. Holland, "Monkey See," *National Geographic*, March 2010.

14. Lara Salahi, "Stem Cell–Engineered Windpipe for Cancer Patients," ABC News, August 2, 2010.

15. Juli Berwald, "Ox Redux," *National Geographic*, July 2010.

16. "Merging Man and Machine," *National Geographic*, January 2010.

17. Gary Anthes, "Future Watch: A.I. comes of age," *Computerworld*, January 26, 2009.

18. Kaku, *Physics of the Future*, 6.

19. Jeffrey S. Passel and D'Vera Cohn, "U.S. Population Projections: 2005–2050," Pew Research Center, February 11, 2008.

CHAPTER 2

Why Missional, Why Now?

Like a person diagnosed with a serious illness following a long period of declining health, many churches across the United States are becoming increasingly aware that they are in peril.[1] Most respond to this realization in predictable ways. Some become angry and look for someone to blame; unfortunately, the pastor is too often the first person in line. Church members speculate that if they had a pastor who was a more spectacular preacher, with better leadership skills or with greater ability to connect with younger adults, then the church would revive, gain new members, and return to former glory days. Many churches respond by working harder at events that once bore fruit, such as youth and children's ministries, special programs, or elaborate worship services. Yet even with these additional efforts, new people do not come to church, join, and stay. Some congregations live in denial, believing that if they remain faithful, people will come to their senses and return to church. None of these approaches address the real problem. Churches are declining because the majority of U.S. Americans are choosing a secular lifestyle, which no longer includes church attendance, and that trend is expected to increase in coming years.

Where is the hope for churches facing this unprecedented rate of cultural change? Our greatest hope is in the life-giving gospel of Jesus Christ, and our next greatest is in the church's long heritage of adapting to meet challenges. Consider, for example, the very early adaptation recorded in Acts 10–11. The Jewish followers of Jesus struggled to accept Gentiles into their understanding of God's redemptive work, but they did adjust, making it possible for the gospel to be shared across the Roman Empire. Even in modern times, there have been great upheavals over new practices, many of which are standard today, such as choirs, organs, and Sunday school. Today, however, we are faced with a new challenge: several generations of young people raised with computers, video games, MTV, YouTube, and smartphones, but with very little knowledge of the Christian gospel or experience with the church. So how is the church adapting today to the challenge of reaching a population that does not have church in their life script at all?

Responses to Change

In his book *The New Conspirators*,[2] Tom Sine identifies four major experimental movements taking place in American Christianity: monastic, emergent, multicultural, and missional. The *monastic movement* appeals to persons seeking the spiritual life. These spiritual explorers sometimes live in loosely gathered communities that place a high value on nurturing their discovery of God, with little formal instruction or requirements for participation. The *emergent movement* is largely a youth culture experience that lives up to its name, with unstructured worship that allows many expressions of spontaneous praise such as art, dance, poetry, and music. Structured discipleship training is limited. Rather, they trust in discipleship relationships to form organically under the inspiration of the Spirit. Intentional *multicultural communities*, in which persons from different backgrounds and ethnicities gather together, reflect a desire to more accurately portray God's kingdom on earth as it is in heaven, and a commitment to multicultural dialogue as a foretaste of God's design for humanity. The fourth trend is the *missional movement*, which is comprised of Christians who believe the gospel of Jesus was intended to have practical impact on the world, as the first fruits of God's coming total restoration in the new heaven and new earth.

Christians in the missional movement choose to become actively involved in alliances with their community. Their involvement attests to their faith that acting on the truth of Christ's gospel makes a difference in the world and demonstrates God's Good News. As a result, they form authentic relationships with others— Christian and non-Christian—while addressing community problems. These efforts lead to true partnerships in which love, respect, and dialogue can arise as a natural part of working together. Community involvement is viewed as a testimony of God's love for people. As the book of James says, "Faith by itself, if it is not accompanied by action, is dead. . . . I will show you my faith by my deeds" (James 2:17-18).

As churches across the land become increasingly aware of the massive cultural changes around them, they are asking, "How can we fit in with God's work now?" The missional movement is one way Christians are responding, by becoming involved with people outside the church to live out the gospel of Jesus Christ. The Missional Church Learning Experience (MCLE) was designed to offer a road map for churches who want to practice community involvement as an expression of their faith. MCLE offers churches a simple step-by-step process to build mission

"The MCLE helps churches discover that they are not alone in their challenges and they are able to spark each other's creativity when looking to meet the needs in their communities. Helping churches move their mind-set from 'come to church' to 'take the church to the streets' will be key to their future."
—Rev. Joan Friesen, Executive Minister, American Baptist Churches of Greater Indianapolis

teams that display healthy, repeatable patterns for partnership with the community.

Historical Christianity and the Missional Movement

Jesus came with a message that was more than mere words; he backed up his claim to divine authority with miracles that no one could do apart from God's power. John's Gospel calls these miracles signs of the kingdom of God that demonstrate God's restoring will for humankind. Jesus then discipled people into the way of God by choosing followers from among the people, who were living under harsh conditions, and sending them to deliver the message of the kingdom of God in words and deeds of healing (Luke 9:1-6). Those who responded to Jesus were transformed from the oppressed and exploited to powerful representatives of God. Christ's resurrection confirmed for them God's ability to complete the promise of a restored creation. They believed the new heaven and new earth would be populated by those who put their faith in God, a faith demonstrated by reflecting God's life-giving nature. These early Christians experienced miracles as God worked among them, many of which are recorded in the book of Acts. They invited others to shift their loyalties from the authorities of this world to the authority of God, and to receive citizenship in the new reality bought for them by Christ.

This realignment with God's authority and vision of Christians as God's ambassadors continued down through the centuries. Worldwide, Christians have been at the forefront of many of humanity's greatest advancements in the last two thousand years. Christians, motivated by their faith, created many of the first hospitals and orphanages and worked toward advancements and achievements in science and the arts. Great modern heroes such as Mother Teresa and Dr. Martin Luther King Jr. made it clear that they expected Christianity to have a powerful effect here and now. Today the missional movement attempts to continue this long heritage of involvement with the world as declared in Christ's prayer: "Your kingdom come, your will be done, *on earth* as it is in heaven" (Matthew 6:10, emphasis added).

The Appeal of Missional Christianity in the Twenty-first Century

The world is enamored with science and technology. Throughout the twentieth century people began shifting their expectation from God as savior to science as the solution for humanity's future. This trend continues today, but science's image has been tarnished as scientific advances increase at an ever-amazing rate without solving our most basic—and ever-increasing—global problems. Today's teens and young adults hold both great hope that humankind will come together as one for the common good, and also great terror at the very real possibility that human corruption and science gone askew will lead to horrors unimagined by prior generations. It is a difficult time to be young, as the beliefs that once held their parents and grandparents steady are now giving way like pebbles on the edge of a cliff. While their search for meaningful answers has opened them to various ideologies, it also offers an opportunity for the gospel of Jesus Christ to be reflected into their lives through living examples. The missional movement exhibits the following qualities that fit the positive values of today's youth and young adults who are searching for hope.

"Without the MCLE, I would have stayed on the sidelines instead of reaching out into my community to assist (in even a small way) those struggling through job loss and tough economic times. As a result of our missional involvement, I continue to volunteer weekly and know God is using me to help others."
—Coleen Remick, member of First Baptist Church, Indianola, IA

■ Creative: The missional movement invites people to explore their passionate interests and participate in making a positive difference in the world. As computers and communications vastly expand our horizons, the potential to be creative sits at our fingertips. No longer restricted to a set regimen for religion, education, or work, people are finding new ways to express their distinctiveness. Being creative helps persons identify themselves on a planet of over seven billion people. Any outlet for creativity that is readily available has great potential to involve people. Can the church give leadership to this desire? Rather than pigeonholing persons into set roles of service, the church can become the leader in helping people identify their potential and supporting their development in Christ's service in a wide array of venues.

■ Networked: The wonder of the Internet is its decentralized and networked nature. Action no longer requires permission through a defined chain of command. Access to the World Wide Web instantly connects a person to almost any resource anywhere in the world. Have an idea for a business or cause? Put it on the Web and find a whole world of connections ready to encourage—no application required. The missional movement captures the energy of its participants in a similar manner by allowing Christians to connect with others inside and outside the faith with whom they share some facet of life. Collaborators can offer ideas and opportunities, and experiment with options for service, without having to make their way through lengthy bureaucratic procedures. An example of networking happened when nine-year-old Rachel Beckwith decided to use her birthday money to buy clean water for fifteen people through a reputable charity. She was trying to collect $300 for the task when tragedy struck and she was killed in a traffic accident. Her story went "viral" on the Web, and within days people had given more than $1 million in her name to bring clean water to people living in Africa.[3]

■ Relational: The missional movement allows people to link their efforts with those of others, creating small groups of highly valued relationships. Relationships remain the key to sharing and building faith, but in the missional movement those relationships are formed while serving a common purpose. Since a shared task usually involves shared values and language, serving together creates a unique opportunity for a trusting relationship to form and fosters the continued contact needed to help it grow.

■ Empowering: The missional movement empowers people to address problems related to their values. With an array of social problems increasingly competing for our awareness, individuals can easily become overwhelmed to the point of apathy. Yet apathy itself diminishes a person. It is life-giving when a person is able to actually do something to make a difference about an unjust situation. The missional movement provides ways for individuals to be a part of the solution to one problem while encouraging their participation in future problem-solving efforts.

■ Transcendent: The missional movement connects people to something that is much bigger than themselves and that has lasting value. Without dictating the terms of another's faith development, the missional movement encourages people to explore how their personal interests fit in with God's restorative mission and to learn with others during their experimentation. Being missional means being a part of God's greater plan for the world and learning more about yourself, God, and others as you become involved.

"We have learned that even as a small church we can make a difference in our community. The MCLE helped us see the possibilities and put them into action."
—First Baptist Church, Anamosa, IA

As recently as eight years ago, a Google search for the word *missional* would not have yielded a single entry. Now a search would generate over 800,000 listings.[4] Only time will tell whether this expanding interest is an indication of the Holy Spirit moving among God's people to facilitate a new era in Christian development. Regardless, the missional movement has captured the imagination of many.

Key Points

■ Our greatest hope is in the life-giving gospel of Jesus Christ, and our next greatest is in the church's long heritage of adapting to meet challenges.

■ The Missional Church Learning Experience (MCLE) was designed to offer a road map for churches that want to practice community involvement as an expression of their faith.

■ It is a difficult time to be young, as the beliefs that once held their parents and grandparents steady are now giving way like pebbles on the edge of a cliff.

■ The missional movement invites people to explore their passionate interests and participate in making a positive difference in the world.

■ Collaborators can offer ideas and opportunities, and experiment with options for service, without having to make their way through lengthy bureaucratic procedures.

■ Relationships remain the key to sharing and building faith, but in the missional movement those relationships are formed while serving a common purpose.

Notes

1. Tom Elrich, "Bad News, Good News," *Morning Walk* (blog), Morning Walk Media, September 16, 2010, www.morningwalk media.com/morning-walk-media-blog/bad-news-good-news.

2. Tom Sine, *The New Conspirators* (Downers Grove, IL:

InterVarsity Press, 2008), 31–55.

3. Amy Harris and J.B. Wogan, "Rachel Beckwith's legacy: $1 million for charity," *The Seattle Times*, August 12, 2011.

4. John Addison Dally, *Choosing the Kingdom* (Herndon, VA: The Alban Institute, 2008), 5.

"Our greatest lesson learned with the MCLE is that the church is *not* the building, but 'out there.' We have the privilege of joining where God is already working! The missional movement has opened the eyes of many in the church. The old way of doing church, expecting people to come to us, is changing. God is working in the minds and hearts of our church family to look out beyond ourselves—with no strings attached."

—Parchment Valley Baptist Church, Ripley, WV

"The MCLE challenges churches to be the people God has called them to be by providing a process for churches to move into this often uncharted territory of community involvement. The safe and supportive environment of the MCLE learning community invites churches to share both their struggles and triumphs with others who are experiencing a similar *reorientation* of vision and priorities."

—Rev. Soozi Whitten Ford, Executive Minister, American Baptist Churches of Indiana and Kentucky

CHAPTER 3

Session 1 —
Getting Started on the Future

When the church teams arrive for Session 1 of the Missional Church Learning Experience (MCLE), there is the usual hum of conversation as people gather, especially around the coffee pot and snacks. The local coordinator leads an opening worship to remind us of the central focus for Christians—Jesus Christ. As the MCLE facilitator begins, people listen expectantly and somewhat skeptically to determine if this event will be worth their time and if it will provide some real potential for their churches' ministries. The facilitator sets the pace for the adventure with these words:

> Congratulations—you have been chosen to serve God at a time unlike any other in human history. You are doing something no human beings have ever done before. You are living through the most accelerated rate of change in human experience. And God has placed you in this time to be transition agents from a Christian heritage we knew and understood to a future that we cannot even imagine. We are here to think about and participate in forming the future of the Christian faith. You have ten seconds to find a partner—someone new to you—to play the Change Game.

The room explodes as people clamor to find a partner, and with that beginning, we jump into the MCLE. No long introductions, no stories about the facilitator's background, only one focus: serving God in our time with the future in mind. By the time the Change Game is finished, most people are in awe of the revolution they have experienced in their lifetime (sample "Change Game Results" can be found in Appendix B, page 101). Many realize they have never before added all the pieces of change together into one picture, and they are relieved to finally understand the source of the uneasiness they are experiencing in these hectic times. We finish the game by discussing the greatest change in the U.S. Christian church in the last fifty years: the staggering drop in the percentage of people who regularly attend church. As we take our seats and catch our collective breath, we consider the question, "How could we fall so far, so fast?" A brief historical review of the changes in the church in the United States during those years helps answer the question. We trace the church's recent history

■ from the small town and rural churches that served as the center of community life in the 1940s;

■ to the rapid rise of suburban churches during the 1950s and 1960s, when tens of thousands of new churches were built to reach growing suburban families;

■ to the high dropout rate of young adults from church life in the 1970s and 1980s, and the adoption of contemporary worship by some churches to attract them back.

In all of these transitions we notice one strong quality: the church has always adapted to change. While understanding the change that has happened is important for the church, it should not be our main focus. When change happened at a slower pace, periods of stability between change cycles gave people time to adapt and determine a new status quo. The discomfort of change causes most of us to avoid change for as long as possible and then, when change occurs, to seek stability as quickly as possible. In today's accelerating rate of change, however, if a person or a group tries to establish a new "normal" by adjusting to changes that have already occurred, they will be overcome by the onward movement of rapid change and caught in a vicious cycle, always falling further and further behind. That is what has happened for many of today's churches.

In Session 1, this idea is demonstrated by having a volunteer play the role of "Change" personified. She or he is instructed to travel throughout the room at will, dodging and weaving at different speeds. While Change moves about, the facilitator, representing the church, tries to keep up. The group is then asked, "Where is the church in relationship to Change?" The answer is clearly, "Always behind."

While some congregations are still struggling with the "worship wars," arguing over traditional versus contemporary music, they fail to realize that change in worship styles took place forty years ago. Those four decades represent two full-grown generations who never knew, much less cared, about such matters. Many of today's young adults have never experienced church, and their taste in music is more likely to be rap, heavy metal, or hip-hop than praise songs. For them church is a relic of a bygone era—something their grandparents did "BC": before computers. Today's secular majority is so disconnected from any faith heritage that they cannot be attracted to attend any church regardless of its worship style. They simply have no interest in church for their lives.

It is always tempting to stop at this point in the MCLE process and have a discussion about how the church could or should have responded to this reality. However, it is more important to look into the near future of the Christian church in the United States. Understanding the change that is coming is essential to serving God in the present.

The Change That Is Coming

The Law of Accelerating Returns[1] states that change brings more change at an ever increasing rate. We have entered a time when change will continue to increase exponentially, causing the present to be in constant flux. In this state of constant change, thinking forward becomes an increasingly important skill. This fact is demonstrated in the next part of the Change demonstration. Once again, the volunteer representing Change is asked to move at random about the room. This time, though, the Facilitator (representing the church) observes Change's movements and intercepts, capturing Change in motion. This activity provides a picture of the future-focused church — studying change and intersecting with it by anticipating its movement.

Twenty years ago, it was popular for churches to form vision teams for long-range planning. However, at our current rate of change, such a group would not and could not make any plans that would have value because their planning would be based on outdated historical information. To illustrate this point, consider a planning committee formed in the Middle Ages trying to plan for the 2012 Summer Olympics. Could they have accurately predicted the need for satellite communication, instant replays, millisecond timing, and athletes in sports that did not yet exist? Yet the changes coming to our culture in the near

"I came away from the MCLE with a sense of hope and gratitude to be a part of something much bigger that God is doing among us here in this rapidly changing world. It helps me counter-balance the anxiety and fearful clutching that happens in the church, because people are afraid of losing what they have."
—Rev. Dr. Susan Crane, Henderson Memorial Baptist Church, Farmington, ME

future are projected to be even more substantial than those since the Middle Ages.

For churches to remain part of God's mission now and in the future, they must develop a new approach to thinking and planning, reaching forward to opportunities that are coming. Churches can start practicing this skill by projecting possible upcoming changes, and then planning backward to the present to be ready to optimize the church's response. This concept is introduced in Session 1 with the following exercise.

The learning community spends five minutes brainstorming possible changes coming to the culture in the next fifteen years, considering such trends as the following:

■ Forty-three percent of all children born in the U.S. in 2010 were born to unwed mothers.[2] What will "family" seem like to these people when they are fifteen years older? Where are the opportunities for the church to become significantly involved now?

■ The U.S. population will expand to more than 400 million in the next fifteen years and will become more multicultural.[3] What opportunities for the gospel of Christ will be opened by these shifts?

■ Projected U.S. church attendance in fifteen years is less than 12 percent of the population.[4] How can the church become involved in people's lives *outside* the church with the gospel of Jesus Christ?

■ It is possible that Christians in the U.S. will no longer have church buildings, paid clergy, or denominational resources in fifteen years. How will we, as the body of Christ, continue to have an impact on our culture?

The group spends the next fifteen minutes discussing the question, "What does the church need to be doing today to be preparing Christians for tomorrow?" This is a very difficult exercise and demonstrates how challenging it is to think ahead, especially for a future full of new or unknown variables. This discussion makes the church's dilemma much clearer. All we know is what has happened in the past; therefore, all our planning has been based on past behavior and expectations. The past is moving away from us at such an astounding rate that it is no longer an accurate guide for the future. It is as though we are traveling in a spaceship toward Mars and planning to build our base camp as though we lived on Earth: by cutting down trees for firewood.

At this point in the session we are ready for some common-sense conversation about the future of the church in the U.S., starting with the average ages of our current church generations. The group is asked, "What is the average age of the World War II generation born between 1910–1926?" and then asked how old that group will be in fifteen years. Then we turn our attention to the next generation—those born between 1927 and 1945. This generation was too young to serve in World War II, but was profoundly affected by witnessing the United States become a major player in the global epic. (I call them the "Believer generation" because they believed and they built. This amazing group believed in institutions and authority. They were the first generation to go to college in large numbers. They built great companies like IBM, GM, and Xerox. They even sent us to the moon using slide rules.)

"I cannot begin to explain to you the excitement that is building. This is exactly what I was looking for in my new pastoral setting: something to get the people excited and involved. I look forward with great anticipation to being a part of this process. I know God is going to bless through this, which in turn will add to the Kingdom and the Great Commission."
—Rev. George E. Murphy, Mt. Vernon Baptist Church, Brownton, WV

Again we consider their average age today and what it will be in fifteen years. And here comes a sobering reality: these two generations—the WWII and Believer generations—are the last two generations with a majority of individuals practicing regular church attendance and tithing (giving 10 percent of their income to their local church).

Next we consider the "Boomer" generation. They were born between 1946 and 1964 and are no longer young. The oldest members of this group are reaching their mid-sixties. How old will they be in fifteen years? Fewer than a third of Boomers attend church regularly, and in spite of their overall increase in personal income compared to their parents and grandparents, their average giving to the local church is only 2.59 percent[5]—and that statistic was in effect before the current downturn of the economy. Many Boomers do not have enough working years left to recover from their substantial losses to retirement.

How are the Boomers' children and grandchildren practicing their faith? In spite of the largest expenditure in Christian youth ministry in history, the return on that investment is not evident among Generation X (born between 1965 and 1982). How many adults under forty-five years of age attend your church? Even if your church does have a good percentage of young adults, it is telling to compare that number to the total population of young adults under forty-five in the community. One young pastor in Clinton, Iowa, took that challenge and discovered that only 4 percent of people under age forty-five in his community attended church. In fifteen years, this generation will be between forty-five and sixty years of age and at least for now, they are not attending church in significant numbers. Nor are they raising their children with any significant contact with the Christian faith.

The statistics grow even dimmer for the Millennial generation (1983–1999) and the iGeneration of children born in the year 2000 and beyond. The bottom line for many churches in the

United States is that in fifteen years, the World War II and Believer generations will no longer be available in sufficient numbers to support local church ministries. The Boomers will be seventy-five to eighty years of age with a minority of them regularly attending church or giving significant amounts of financial support. All this, along with the vast majority of the next generations not attending or financially supporting churches, raises the question, "What percentage of today's churches will continue in fifteen years?"

Now is the time to be asking an important question, namely, "What is the purpose of the church?" Is the purpose to retain an increasingly smaller subculture until Jesus returns? Or is the purpose of the church to be involved with God in the mission of restoring the world, turning it right-side up with the gospel of Jesus Christ? Consider the following concept from chaos theory: when an increasingly complex system can no longer sustain itself, even the smallest concentrated effort by a committed few can change the direction of the many.[6] Armed with God's love, should not Christians have the potential for the most powerful effect on any culture? Is it conceivable that God is preparing the church to be effective in new ways, which requires dismantling the old delivery system in order to move us toward new forms of effectiveness?

As discussed in Chapter 2, Christians throughout the country are asking these questions and experimenting with different responses, including the missional church movement. Missional churches shift their primary ministry focus from inside the walls of the church to outward involvement with their communities, demonstrating the

"The MCLE gave us much to think about and it will take time for us to digest the information, although I do believe we are well on our way . . . "
—Leslie Miller, member of Eastwood Baptist Church, Medford, OR

Good News of Jesus Christ in word and deed, delivered in loving relationships. As churches explore this change in ministry focus, they find it offers traditional churches two advantages. First, community involvement aligns with their understanding that the gospel was always meant to have practical application in this world. Second, churches can begin experimenting with the change toward more outward-focused ministry with the community while still maintaining parts of their traditional church life. Exploring the missional movement begins with a study of its essential principles. Therefore Session 1 of the MCLE begins there as well.

Main Missional Ideas

Every stage of development in Christian history has been driven by main ideas that define its focus. Session 1 of the MCLE introduces four main ideas that are foundational to the missional church movement. After each idea is introduced, the teams take time to complete a survey and score themselves on how well their church is currently demonstrating that quality. The facilitator keeps the surveys and returns them to the teams at the final session, so that they may determine for themselves how much understanding they have gained from their missional practice of being involved with their communities. The four main ideas presented are as follows.

1. God is on a mission of total restoration.

Setting things right is the very nature of God. The missional movement joins German missiologist Karl Hartenstein in expressing this concept with the term *missio Dei*[7] (Latin for "mission of God" or "sending of God"), in which mission is understood as being derived from the very nature of God. Going back to the image given in Genesis, humans were created to enjoy good relationships with God, with others, and with the rest of the created world. The missional movement is about capturing God's passion for restoring the lost relationships between humanity and God, as well as among people themselves. It also involves a complete restoration of creation as an expression of God's creative goodness.

For humans to fit in with this mission, we must first understand that the mission is God's from beginning to end. God initiated this reclamation, brought it to us through Jesus, and invites us to get involved by serving. God is sustaining this continued mission throughout human history, and God has the intent and power to fulfill this beautiful restoration in the physical reality of the "new heaven and new earth" depicted in Revelation 21–22. By understanding the centrality of God in the mission of restoration, we can correctly understand our part in it—avoiding pride by thinking we can bring it about, and avoiding despair over current conditions.

2. Everyone is invited to joyfully join God in the mission.
There is an interesting story in the Gospel of Luke (9:49-50), where a person who was not a part of Jesus' disciples was working miracles. The disciples tell Jesus, "We tried to stop him, because he is not one of us," to which Jesus replied, "Whoever is not against you is for you." First the Jews, and then the Christians, made the mistake of understanding God's mission as belonging exclusively to

"During this time of financial crisis, survival mentality is a temptation. Rather than stressing scarcity of resources, the MCLE promotes an appreciation of the abundance of God's provision. Our churches need this training to look beyond themselves for partnership in their communities for doing the work of Christ. These alliances can breathe new life into our congregations as they discover new connections with people in the community who care about people."
—Rev. Alan Shumway, First Baptist Church, Belfast, ME

them and being only for them. This way of thinking creates a separatist mentality of "us versus them."

The missional movement attempts to grasp a greater reality—that God is God of all, whether that truth is recognized or not, and that God's mission of restoration is open to any who choose to be a part of God's goodness, even when it is not fully understood. One of the most staggering effects of the missional movement upon Christians is the realization that other people are not simply targets to be converted to their expression of Christianity, but rather that God brings new life to humans as they engage with God and find their value. It is through collaborative efforts with others who are serving in God's restorative mission that Christians experience renewed vitality of their own faith by seeing God at work in the world. They also begin to value people they may not have previously known.

Thus begins the understanding that John 3:16 is not complete without the message of John 3:17; that God loves the world so much that God came to us in Jesus, not to condemn, but to save. For some Christians this is the most significant aspect in the missional movement: God's open invitation to everyone to become involved with God in the mission of restoration and, in so doing, to begin to know God. Yet even a quick scan of Jesus' life finds that his ministry portrays this truth. Time and again Jesus chose disciples from those whom others cast away—tax collectors, fishermen, the Samaritan woman, a Gadarene demoniac, and a little boy with a lunch of fish and bread that fed thousands.

3. Serving in God's mission follows "the Way" demonstrated by Jesus.

God's revelation through Jesus contains qualities that demonstrate God's missional nature. First, we see in Jesus the pattern of God coming to us. God did not wait for humanity to come seeking a restored relationship. This action teaches us that, to be on mission with God, we must go into the world and not wait for the world to come to our churches seeking Christ.

Second, in Jesus we notice that not only does God initiate the contact, but God comes to us in a form we can understand. God comes to us in human form, communicating in words, stories, and daily examples that make comprehension simple. God wants to communicate! Therefore, to serve in God's mission we must find ways to communicate that are effective and convenient to others living in our culture.

Third, the message that Jesus delivered about God was accurate about God's nature and God's will for humanity. Jesus offered a clear choice to each of us: to be restored to God and participate in the restoration or reject God's gift of grace. Similarly, we must be able to explain Jesus' Good News clearly and completely, and to do that we must understand it ourselves.

Fourth, Jesus demonstrated God's will and God's way by changing people's reality. He healed, fed, touched, and even raised the dead. Most of us feel unable to do such wonderful things, but all together we could do a lot more than we currently are doing.

Fifth, Jesus did not just talk about God, nor did he stop with making changes in people's reality. Instead, Jesus delivered both

"The MCLE challenged us to think of being the church in new and creative ways, and provided not only models for that but opportunities to experiment with what it meant to be the church in the world. Participating was a morale-booster to many in our congregation as well, and the community project we developed was an eye-opening experience as well as a point of pride for our community. We are grateful for the privilege of participating and the leadership that was provided."
—Community Baptist Church, Truman, MN

word and deed in a deeply personal, loving relationship. Jesus is the true representation of God. In the same way, people who are on mission with God and involved in the restoration must display God in word, deed, and loving relationship.

4. Followers of Jesus are found in the world and formed through service.

Week after week, Christians hold worship services in churches where fewer and fewer come to hear the Christian gospel. Yet, in truth, waiting for people to come to him was not Jesus' model for making disciples. In almost every story in the Gospels, we see Jesus out in the world, meeting people in their daily routine and inviting them to become a part of God's reign in their current circumstances. The future of faith development in the U.S. may reflect this pattern of Jesus. As Christians in the missional movement spend more of their time involved with the struggle for restoring goodness in their communities, they may naturally draw others toward relationship with God through Christ. First Peter 3:15 advises us to be ready to give the reason for our hope with a gentle and respectful response.

A related pattern distinguished in Jesus' ministry is that he immediately put every new disciple to work in God's mission. Most of us learn best by doing. Jesus demonstrated this by sending out his brand-new disciples to villages he had yet to visit and telling them to proclaim God's reign and to heal (see Luke 10:1-17). In a similar way, followers of Jesus will form more quickly and mature in their faith more deeply by serving God through serving others and by having a safe, loving place to return to, where they can reflect on what they learned in the process. This new/old form of discipleship works well with today's young adults, who have instant access to the world through the Internet and are not willing to wait months or even years sitting through our traditional classroom models of Christian training before getting to taste the action.

Each session of the MCLE revisits these main missional ideas at increasingly deeper levels as the participants reflect on their experiences with community involvement. The church teams are reminded that there are no experts for where we are going. They are the people God has chosen to be transition agents from our faith heritage of the past to someone else's Christian experience in the future. They are advised that during Session 3 they will be invited to write their own missional ideas, adding their ideas to the efforts of others.

Learning Community Covenant

The final portion of Session 1 is used to create a Learning Community Covenant, a process that requires defining the term "covenant." We live in a contract world where two parties make a contract when they exchange something of value. If either party fails to perform, the contract is broken—a standard which leads to a lot of broken contracts and broken relationships as a result. In a covenant relationship, both parties agree to do what is right, because it is right. Even if one party fails, the other does their best to keep their commitment for the good of the whole. Part of being a missional people is living our faith in a way that benefits the whole world. For this reason each learning community creates a covenant among themselves reflecting the values and commitments that are important to them.

Building the Learning Community Covenant begins with clearly stating the expectation of the MCLE process. It is not about selling the missional movement, and church teams are advised that their church will not become transformed into a missional church by simply participating in the MCLE. Rather, the MCLE is an introduction to the missional movement, an invitation for Christian churches to explore together one way God may be preparing us for continued mission in this time of continual change. Next, the dates for the remaining sessions are written into the covenant and the content of each session is reviewed so that each team can commit to participation for the good of the group. The four steps in the MCLE process, which form the foundation for assignments between Sessions 1 and 2, are introduced (Appendix C, p. 108). The steps will aid the church teams in designing a small interactive community project, which they will use to practice the missional principles. The steps will be introduced in detail during follow-up technology sessions. Finally, the group gathers for a covenanting ceremony to finish the day, allowing each church team to express their hopes for their church's future.

While the MCLE Session 1 is a good beginning toward becoming a learning community, the churches do not yet have enough investment in one another to deeply care about the others' outcomes. That comes with time, shared experiences, and the work of God's Spirit. Since one of the keys to building any relationship is regular contact, we build the learning community through regular follow-up, including two technology sessions between each in-person session, to offer encouragement and explanations and to share experiences.

Key Points

■ In today's accelerating rate of change, if a person or a group tries to establish a new "normal" by adjusting to changes that have already occurred, they will be overcome by the onward movement of rapid change and caught in a vicious cycle, always falling further and further behind.

■ The past is moving away from us at such an astounding rate that it is no longer an accurate guide for the future. For churches to remain part of God's mission, thinking forward to opportunities that are coming becomes an increasingly important skill.

■ Today's secular majority is so disconnected from any faith heritage that they cannot be attracted to attend any church regardless of its worship style. To be on mission with God we must go into the world and not wait for the world to come to our churches seeking Christ.

■ The missional movement is about capturing God's passion for restoring the lost relationships between humanity and God, among people, and with creation. The movement attempts to grasp the reality that God is God of all and that God's mission of restoration is open to any who choose to be a part of God's goodness.

■ Through collaborative efforts with others who are serving in God's restorative mission, Christians see God at work in the world and experience renewed vitality. Followers form more quickly and faith matures more deeply by serving God through serving others, and by having a safe place to reflect on what they are learning.

Notes

1. Ray Kurzweil, "The Law of Accelerating Returns," www.kurzweilai.net/the-law-of-accelerating-returns.

2. ABC National News, August 2010.

3. Jeffrey S. Passel and D'Vera Cohn, "U.S. Population Projections: 2005–2050," Pew Research Center, February 11, 2008.

4. David T. Olson, *The American Church in Crisis* (Grand Rapids: Zondervan, 2008), 39.

5. Tom Sine, *The New Conspirators* (Downers Grove, IL: InterVarsity Press, 2008), 206.

6. Ervin Laszlo, *The Chaos Point: The World at the Crossroads* (Charlottesville, VA: Hampton Roads, 2006), opening page.

7. John G. Flett, *The Witness of God: The Trinity, Missio Dei, Karl Barth, and the Nature of Christian Community* (Grand Rapids: Eerdmans, 2010), 124.

CHAPTER 4

Session 2—
Building Healthy,
Repeatable Patterns

In the four months between the first and second sessions of the MCLE, the church teams involved in the learning community work on several assignments based on a four-step process (Appendix C, pp. 108–117) to help them practice missional principles. Engagement and retention levels typically remain high because the learning community's coordinator and MCLE facilitator remain in continuous communication during this interim period, which includes two technology-based sessions that help explain the four-step process. Thus, Session 2 is always a hopeful time as the teams gather and realize they are still moving forward together. Once again, worship is the first activity of the session to remind us that "unless the LORD builds the house, the builders labor in vain" (Psalm 127:1).

Session 2 is dedicated to building healthy, repeatable patterns for sustainable missional practice. Such missional practice includes building mission teams that form disciples, learning to listen to the community, looking for ministry partners, and discerning our part in God's restorative mission. We begin the session with this challenge: "If your church launched ten new mission teams that followed your team's example of being involved in God's mission with your community, what qualities would you need to model for them?" It is encouraging to remind the teams that other MCLE churches have already experienced multiplication, and that the potential exists for their congregations to launch multiple mission teams in the future. This picture of the potential of multiplication brings us to the critical first step.

Step 1—Building Our Mission Team: Discipleship Central

According to Matthew 28:19, the purpose of the church is to make disciples of Jesus Christ. Over the centuries Christians have employed a wide variety of methods to train disciples. In modern times, much of discipleship formation has been based on classic classroom education models and most often has occurred inside the church building. In contrast, the missional movement focuses primarily on learning about God and the mission through involvement with the outside community, in demonstrating the love of God. As the culture becomes increasingly secular, the church is finding it necessary to return to the discipleship method used by Christ: finding disciples in the world and forming them through service. Most of us feel ill-equipped for the task. To ease our way into this renewed understanding of nurturing disciples, Step 1 asks the mission teams to form and carry out simple plans in response to two questions:

1. How will their team practice being a Christian community throughout the MCLE?
2. How will the team communicate their MCLE involvement to their church?

Starting with the first question of how the team will practice being a Christian community, we remind ourselves of two reasons why this value is important. First, ministry is hard work and we each need the support provided by the group to help maintain the steady connection with the Holy Spirit that empowers the mission with God. Second, we are modeling the Christian life for others who will join the team's efforts along the way. With these reasons in mind, each team is asked to share examples of practices that are helping them remain faithful to the value of being a Christian community. We discuss possible outcomes, if a mission team from their church was to practice a simple plan for staying Christ-centered throughout their effort. Identified advantages generally range from increased team cohesion to improved spiritual development. In this conversation we first begin to glimpse why God is inviting us to join in God's work outside the church. God disciples us as we get involved. Often we have thought of others as being the target of our discipleship efforts when, in truth, it is God who disciples us all. It is not until we see people as God sees them that we realize we are all travelers, journeying into the experience of knowing God; that is when discipleship develops.

We then consider the alternative—what might happen if the team does *not* experience authentic Christian fellowship while being involved with their community? After all, for some people outside the church, their interaction with the team may be the only example of Christianity they will ever encounter. Others point out that the quality of our faith will show in the quality of our relationships. If we truly want others to become disciples of Jesus, we must first help them form relationships with disciples of Jesus.

This discussion inevitably causes me to reflect on a verse that people are fond of quoting from the book of James: "Faith by itself, if it is not accompanied by action, is dead" (James 2:17). But the opposite is also true, that works without faith is dead. There are many reasons that people become active in a cause, but their motives can easily become self-serving. Christians who make the connection between their service and their relationship with God are not only highly motivated, but can produce results that go far beyond improving a situation or feeling good about their involvement. Their participation with God's life-giving nature deepens relationships and understanding within themselves and between others. Following the exchange of scenarios, the teams then spend a few minutes revisiting their plan for being a Christian community during the MCLE, and they make improvements knowing that their pattern will have an impact on future mission teams from their church.

Moving on to the next exercise, the teams report their plans to communicate their MCLE efforts to their churches. The facilitator reminds them that the teams are not responsible for getting every member in their respective churches involved. They are simply to go through the MCLE process and share their experiences with their congregation. The group identifies some benefits of mission teams communicating well with their churches. The list usually includes the expectations that more people will get involved and that enthusiasm for the mission will grow.

Pressing the communication idea further, we consider the opposite scenario: "What are the possible ramifications if mission teams fail to communicate with their churches?" At this point usually a few eyebrows raise, as people begin to understand that their team is setting a pattern for future teams that may follow them into God's mission with the community. They list some of the disadvantages, such as fewer people involved and an increase in skepticism and conflict. The church teams then spend a few minutes working on their plan to improve communication with their churches

"Ready for a challenge? Ready to make a difference? Ready for a true joyride? Be a part of the Missional Church Learning Experience! God is waiting for you— are you coming?"

—Lisa Simmons, member of First Baptist Church,
Ravenswood, WV

throughout the MCLE process. The group is advised that these two team-building values will be revisited at each session, with the hope that repetition produces repeatable patterns.

All three remaining steps of the MCLE are designed to build healthy patterns for community involvement. Each step invites a variety of creative adaptations. Original expression is encouraged throughout the process, with the belief that ingenuity spurs on the learning community's growth. The church teams are asked to share their experiences and what they learned about their community, themselves, and God as they complete the steps. The responses are always lively and interesting.

Step 2—Learning to Listen to Our Community

Learning to listen is a foundational step toward building any relationship. It shows respect and genuine interest. The mission teams learn that listening is an important part of moving out into their community, an essential step prior to taking any action. The teams explore this value by actually going out into their communities and asking people outside the church about what is on their hearts and minds. Step 2 gives them guidelines to help with the task, but there is plenty of room for variation.

Some teams have expressed shock at how easy it was to talk with people about topics of community concern. Others have had heart-wrenching experiences as people expressed their opinion that the church does not seem to care very much about anyone but its own members, since the neighborhood simply sees people coming and going from the church building but never stopping to get involved in the larger community. Those who have participated in this listening step are glad that they did. To broaden the learning, the facilitator asks, "If your church developed the pattern of regularly listening to the community, what might happen?" Most participants begin to recognize that showing up and asking for the community's thoughts begins to establish a bridge for relationship. Other respondents suggest that regular listening might lead the church to make better decisions about use of resources and more effective ministry efforts.

Now the facilitator flips the question and asks the group, "What are the disadvantages if the church does not listen to the community?" Teams typically begin to recognize this *is* the current practice of many of their churches, resulting in poor participation from the community and missed opportunities. This leads the group to brainstorm ways that community conversations could be built into church life on a regular basis. This exercise ends with a reflective question: "What would be the effect of requiring every church ministry to survey the community *before* starting any ministry venture?" Usually by now, if there are teams who have not yet done Step 2, they cannot wait to give it a try because they have seen the potential that simply learning to listen to the community may have on the church.

Step 3—Looking for Potential Mission
Partners in Our Community

Step 3 is usually good news for churches that feel too small, too old, or too poor to be involved with their communities. Most churches have adopted a belief that to do community mission, the church must provide all the resources of money, energy, and people. One of

"I want to thank you for inspiring us to get out of the boat. We all just got an e-mail from Luis Palau who lives in the Portland area, challenging the churches with the idea that the community must see us as more than a piece of property on the corner. . . . Hmm . . . sounds familiar."

—Rev. Ken Blondeaux, Woodland Park Baptist Church, Portland, OR the most effective aspects of the missional movement is helping Christians understand that just showing up in the community has a positive impact for everyone. Many Christians have never envisioned themselves as being catalysts for change, able to lead by stirring others to be involved in God's restorative mission.

Step 3 invites the teams to simply take a survey of the resources currently available within the community, looking for who is doing what. During this step many church teams come to the realization that the church does not need to "reinvent the wheel." There are many community groups already involved in life-giving efforts that would welcome the church's participation.

Some of the comments from church teams in this section have been amusing. One man told of going to a city council meeting as part of their team's inquiry, and having the mayor so overwhelmed that a church representative had shown up that he asked the man to sit with him on the dais. Another church team told of a mayor's shocked comment, "I've been mayor of this town for sixteen years and you are the first church to ever ask, 'How can we help?'" Never have I heard of any group being offended that Christians have taken an interest in their work, and several teams have found openings where they did not expect them, such as at schools, park districts, city shelters, and even a local strip bar. This is when the MCLE really starts to be fun! As each group tells about their experiences, others get excited to follow their example.

Step 4, Part 1—Discerning Our Part in God's Mission

At this point in Session 2, groups often enter into a time of quiet reflection as we talk about The Call. After learning to listen to the community in Step 2, and seeing what is already going on through Step 3, we are faced with the question of how to respond. The teams' involvement has exposed them to the size and scope of the problems in their communities, and it is natural to feel overwhelmed. Most are unsure about what part to take on and how to get involved, and are even a little afraid of the cost of being involved with people's trouble. How do we decide what to do?

Discerning our part is critical in the missional movement. Christians are accustomed to thinking about a call to ministry as something that only happens to important biblical heroes, such as Moses or David. However, we sometimes need help in recognizing our involvement with God in the world as a holy calling. The teams review the following basic principles for recognizing God's call to involvement:

■ Not every need is a call. Jesus did not heal every leper, feed all who were hungry, or raise all the dead.

■ God alone can clarify in what, where, and with whom we are to get involved. That involves asking God to reveal our part.

■ Our involvement is not for the purpose of ending the problem, but rather to serve as a sign of God's will for restored life and God's power to bring good through the work of ordinary people who are willing to get involved.

■ Only God knows how our part fits into God's great purpose. We cannot and should not judge the effectiveness of our efforts by the known outcome. Every involvement of one human with another has the potential for blessing.

"The MCLE has taken our focus off ourselves and given us a vision for what we can do for others. It is fun to serve and fun to work together. Families like to work together and children are easily incorporated. We like each other better too, as we see the smiles and hear the laughter of the folks gathered to work. We have gained some pride in our church and believe we have something new to give our community."
—First Baptist Church, Charles City, IA

Here are some helpful reminders about the MCLE process:

■ Each team's community engagement is for the purpose of practicing missional principles, so that they can multiply their efforts with other mission teams from their church.

■ A team's effort does not need to be big to be effective. God has blessed small beginnings and knows what might be accomplished with even a mustard seed–sized effort.

■ It is okay to enter into partnership with other groups, even non-Christian groups. Working with non-Christians helps everyone come to know one another and why we serve.

With these reminders in mind, we listen as the church teams explain where they are in their discernment of what God is inviting them to do. The facilitator also suggests that the teams leave room for their plan to change in case they find themselves taken in a different direction along the way. Many MCLE church stories describe starting with one idea that morphed into another. The important point is to release our assumptions and follow God's Spirit. Often this conversation with the learning community feels like a holy moment as we begin to trust one another with our hopes.

Step 4, Part 2—The Community Project Outline

At this point the teams have lots of good ideas, but how do they make these ideas happen? The last section of Session 2 covers the process of building a community project outline. For most, this is the practical kind of planning that is so easily understood but so rarely done. Each team is asked to write their community project outline and send it to the MCLE facilitator and coordinator as a way of helping us help them. Their community project outlines are also shared with the rest of the learning community for prayer support.

The community project outline starts by asking the team to give the community involvement a name. Names are very important. Giving a name helps bring the idea to life and aids the team in talking about their work. Sometimes the names are very creative and even cause the team to improve their vision for the potential of their community engagement. The outline then asks the team to reflect on what they learned while listening to the community during Step 2, and how this project reflects the community's interests. Next the outline asks the team to list community resources they uncovered during Step 3 that might be helpful in their plans. After considering these important inputs from Step 2 and Step 3, the outline walks the team through the standard questions of Who? What? Where? When? How? The guidelines for each question help the team put their process together into a holistic plan. The outline even asks the team how they will celebrate when their project is complete. Putting the process in writing and sharing their outlines with the other teams of their learning community will foster an accountability among the teams that is helpful to bringing the dreams to reality.

As Session 2 concludes, we gather as a community of faith to commit ourselves to mutual support. Each church team takes the center of the circle in turn, as those around them pray for the success of their project and for the spiritual growth of their team between now and the next session. Each church thus receives the blessings of all the others. It is during this time that the churches

"Being part of the MCLE has given our small church the confidence, encouragement, and skills to start a new ministry in partnership with a local nursing home, something we never would have thought of doing before the MCLE process."

—Niantic Baptist Church, Niantic, CT

first begin to identify with each other as companions on an exploratory journey of faith. They begin to care for one another— that moment when God and humans come together to change the world with the love of Jesus Christ.

Key Points

■ Ministry is hard work and we each need the support provided by a group to help maintain the steady connection with the Holy Spirit that empowers the mission with God.

■ It is not until we see people as God sees them that we realize we are all travelers, journeying into the experience of knowing God; that is when discipleship develops.

■ The book of James states that "faith by itself, if it is not accompanied by action, is dead" (James 2:17), but it is also true that works without faith is dead. Through local mission, we model the Christian life for others who will join the team's efforts along the way.

■ Most churches have adopted a belief that to do community mission, the church must provide all the resources of money, energy, and people. However, just showing up in the community has a positive impact for everyone.

■ Many churches will begin with an idea that morphs into another. The important point is to release our assumptions and follow God's Spirit.

CHAPTER 5

Getting Beyond Beginning

After Session 2 the MCLE churches begin the good work of implementing their community involvement plan. However, teams tend to become so focused on the project that they forget the purpose is to practice the missional principles and reflect on that experience. For many years the church has seen its work with the community as charity, often delegated to a few people and moved to the periphery of the church's main focus for ministry, that is, the church itself. How does the church shift its focus outward toward others, not just as a one-time event but as a permanent change in direction for the delivery of the gospel of Jesus Christ? While the first two sessions of the MCLE have laid the groundwork for a broader understanding of the gospel and community involvement, it is during this time of actually working with the community that the teams become most open to understanding God's missional nature and its impact on both church and culture. To maximize this learning period between Session 2 and Session 3, two instructional sessions are delivered via technology. These technology sessions cover multiplying mission teams, which is discussed in this chapter, and change skills, which will be explored in Chapter 6.

Understanding Change Patterns
Change can feel like a rubber band being stretched to its limit and then snapping back to its original shape when released. When

something new stretches us, the change force must continue or else we snap back to our previous condition. Dieting is an example. It usually fails for one of two reasons: either we go into it with a short-term perspective ("I'm going to cut out desserts for two weeks") or we declare for ourselves a new reality that cannot be sustained ("I'm never going to eat dessert again!"). What we need is a better understanding of the change process. Change usually follows a pattern of adoption over an extended time—from event, to trend, to a change of heart and mind, which leads to a change in the structures that support our routines.

The likelihood of sustained growth increases by realizing that, while all change starts with a single event, that event must multiply and grow into a trend for change to continue. A trend represents a change in behavior in an increasing number of people, and often introduces those involved to new thought patterns. During this phase there will be a time of evaluation and resistance, which is normal to the change process. However, as more and more people begin experiencing the multiplying events, they grow in their personal investment and their perspective begins to shift to a new view of reality—a new normal. Usually it is only after the event has become a trend and has begun to change the thinking of the majority of the group that the organizational structure begins to re-form itself around the new mindset. Eventually the structures formed by the change become so entrenched that if they are threatened, major conflicts can erupt.

An historical example of a positive change pattern can be seen in the adoption of Sunday school by many Christian churches. At some point someone either heard or read about Sunday school and thought it sounded like a good idea. That person convinced others until enough people were willing to try leading Sunday school for children. The group enjoyed the event and saw that it had a good impact on reaching children with the Christian gospel, so they decided to offer it again, and then again. At that point some in the church may have noticed the trend and questioned its value, as was the case in many churches where, for example, issues arose about teaching being a secular activity that violated the Sabbath. Eventually, however, the trend prevailed until Sunday school became a regularly scheduled event, causing a whole host of supporting structures to arise to make it more effective, including Sunday school superintendents and Christian Education Committees. These structures often remain in place long after the effectiveness of the effort has waned. However, if someone were to suggest disassembling the structures they would quickly meet resistance because such a change would require people to confront a significant loss.

Understanding these change patterns can give churches a chance to maximize the normal change responses and avoid unnecessary conflicts. The MCLE is designed to give traditional churches an opportunity to experiment with the missional church movement by actually designing and implementing a community engagement plan and reflecting on what they learned, all within the safety of a learning community of other like-minded church teams. That is a one-time event. Additional mission teams must develop in order for others in the church to experience the effect of missional involvement and choose to continue, taking the church to the next level of the change process.

"We announced our MCLE project in our worship service this past Sunday and already we have a woman who has been on the 'fringe' of the church for years tell us how excited she is about the project and how she would love to volunteer! A beginning of some missional church spirit. Hopefully we will see even more!"
—Rev. Jeff Patnaude, Ogunquit Baptist Church, Ogunquit, ME

It is very much like taking a driver's education class. You read the manual, pass the written test, and then get behind the wheel to try it out (hopefully someplace safe). If, however, you then get out of the car and say, "Wow, that was exciting," but never drive again, the purpose will be lost. So it is with the missional movement. It's not enough to learn the ideas, have one good experience, and then walk away, never to interact with your community again. The MCLE teams are advised not to try to persuade others in their church to become missional, but rather to encourage their participation and allow the missional encounters to change the church's expectations. They are also cautioned not to waste effort on reorganizing church structures before the hearts and minds of the church members are prepared by a wide acceptance of missional experience and reflection.

Multiplying Mission Teams

To get from an event to a trend, one experience with community engagement must expand into more. Back to the dieting example, say you cut out desserts for two weeks and you like the change. It may be only a small change, but still, it's nice to fit into your jeans a little better. What happens now? How do you keep going? The following discussion provides thoughts on how teams can bring the values practiced in the MCLE assignments to the whole congregation.

Make Listening a Priority

How do we stay attuned to God? One way is by making listening a priority. And one of the ways we can hear God is through listening to those around us. What is on the hearts and minds of the people outside the church who live in our community? What might we learn about ourselves, God, and others if we made listening a regular priority? To get motivated, ask your church leadership two questions: What advantages would there be to the church if we listened to the community on a regular basis? What disadvantages would there be to the church if we didn't listen to the community regularly? Next, brainstorm together ways that the church could begin to listen to the community. Ideas could include prayer walks, hand-delivered invitations, small gifts, acts of service, or short surveys—anything that gets your church out into the community where they can listen and learn. Pick one approach, do it, review the experience to see what you learned, and make plans for the next community listening experience. Don't worry about doing something big or elaborate; just do something to get started. The very act of listening will itself have impact on your community and your church. Imagine a church that cares enough about people to ask for their opinion. Before long, opportunities for community involvement will abound!

Look for Potential Ministry Partners

God is active in our surroundings all the time, and sometimes we find God at work in people and places that would surprise most Christians. After all, Jesus shocked the religious people of his time with his choice of company. Invite church leaders or other interested parties to consider whom God is already working with in your city or town to bring God's healing love. It can be a simple thing to survey the resources in your community on a regular basis. Even an annual inquiry into community resources would begin to help your church see the trends and changes that are happening in your environment. Simple tools like the city or county website, local papers, or the yellow pages (if you still have one)

"Many thanks for the MCLE training sessions. They were awesome and I am truly excited about what God will have us do in the coming months!"
—Rev. Dylon Young, Miracle Hills Church, Omaha, NE

can all bring in new information. Bring the list of what is going on in your community to your church's attention and invite prayer and reflection on what the information reveals about your community's condition.

It's important to understand that God is not waiting on us to do God's restoration mission. If we won't play, others will. God has proved this over and over again, even as Jesus chose "tax collectors and sinners" rather than religious leaders to reveal God's power. If we develop the habit of regularly reviewing what is happening in our community, we will know who else is already serving and what they are doing. We will then be much better prepared to recognize potential ministry partners and to join God in this restoration work in our community. Who knows what new insights we may gain by partnering with those whom God is inviting us to join?

Discover the Passion

I believe God forms the passions within each person that direct us to our part in God's great work. The church that learns to listen for the passion expressed by people both inside and outside the church will find the source of limitless energy for ministry. What topics create interest? These reveal where the heart lives, and the passion of even one person who has been moved by a need can inspire others. The church can help by encouraging people to pay attention to what moves them and by teaching them how to discern a call to God's work in their lives. By taking their interests seriously, the church is acknowledging that people's entire lives—not just their church participation—comprise their Christian life and service. The church that teaches, recognizes, encourages, and supports the discernment of calling in people's lives will become a catalytic agency in the community, known throughout the area as a church that is invested in developing people. Some ways that churches can encourage the recognition of God's call are by teaching and preaching call stories from the Bible; arranging visits from missionaries, both national and international, to talk about how they received their call to ministry; inviting local social agencies to speak to the church; and hosting local community fairs where representatives from various community services speak about their work and invite people to form teams of responders to partner with local agencies and connect that work with the church. Once you begin to think of your community as God's mission field and your church as God's partner with others, the supply of resources and contacts seems endless.

Build on What People Are Already Doing

Churches are filled with people who are already actively involved in their community but who do not connect their efforts to their Christian lives. Rather than trying to get everyone to give all their time to the church's schedule of activities, the church can begin to recognize God's call at work in the people through their interests outside the church. The church can partner in their efforts by helping individuals learn to invite others, both inside and outside the church, to come alongside them, forming mission teams. Being missional helps move people from individual efforts to being a part of a team. As they begin to see their involvement as part of God's discipleship in their lives, they will have a broader understanding of discipleship, which will also help them recognize discipleship opportunities for others. Far too often we think that we make disciples, rather than recognizing that as God's work. It is important to recall the words of Jesus as recorded in John 15:16: "You did

"It is good to see our MCLE teams come together and explore new avenues. You have stimulated much food for thought."
—Rev. Dr. Joyce B. Duerr, Tabernacle of Hope,
Fiskeville, RI

not choose me, but I chose you and appointed you so that you might go and bear fruit—fruit that will last."

One way churches can promote a team-building culture is by encouraging exploration teams when someone offers an idea for service. During the MCLE, when anyone expresses a good idea for service, we have fun chanting the response, "*Great*, where's your team?" For churches that use this idea, anyone who would like to consider an idea for ministry can form an exploration team. The person is instructed to invite a few people to help research the idea using the four steps of the MCLE: build the team to be Christ-centered, listen to the community, look for potential partners, and discern God's will for the ministry idea. The exploration teams can be encouraged to "register" their exploration with the church leaders for prayer and to report back what they learn with any suggestions for going forward. This gives the church a process to encourage idea development without having to oversee every exploration. Often in the process of developing an exploration team, a new ministry does come forth and the team is already in development. Sometimes a MCLE participant will object, "Well, this could get messy if we're not all doing the same thing at the same time." Yes, this is true. Being missional can be very messy. If your church defines its ministry as having everyone share the same experience, then exploration teams are not for your church. However, if your church defines its mission as calling everyone—both people inside and outside the church—into service with God, then the more mission opportunities, the better. Only your church can discern your call to service in God's mission.

Another way to encourage the connection between people's volunteer work and the church is to post a list of all the community activities that your members participate in (e.g., Habitat for Humanity, food bank) and ask if they would be willing to serve as points of contact for others who might share that interest. This can be done on church websites or in monthly newsletters. Churches that do this are often amazed by how far-reaching their church members' efforts are within the community. It helps the church realize they already have a missional spirit and a presence within the community. This gives the church motivation to continue.

Ask God . . .

God knows exactly which efforts fit into the development of the person, team, church, and community, and which are distractions. Prayer is the obvious way to discern what to do, when to do it, and with whom. But many Christians are better at talking about the importance of prayer than actually practicing it. Making prayer a priority when establishing your mission teams will help incorporate this source of power and communication with God. Prayer creates the essential relationship necessary to hear God in times of choice. Often in the MCLE process we hear stories of teams who were stuck because of too much information, overwhelming need, and no agreement between team members. Most often when those teams run smack into a brick wall of defeat and turn to prayer, it is then that we hear stories of breakthroughs that put them on a path of community involvement. And sometimes the path turns out to be very different than the one they expected. We share a joke in the MCLE learning community: "How do we discern God's will? . . . Any way we can!" There's a lot of truth to that humor. The one assurance we can have as Christians is that if we want to please God and we ask how we can be of service, God will find a way to communicate with us.

"Back in 2008, our church decided to become involved in the MCLE because we figured there must be more we could do for our community. Through the missional training, we decided we could really make a difference."
—North Foster Baptist Church, Foster, RI

Take Your Ministries Outside the Walls

By now you may be asking the question, "How do I get my church started on the missional path?" The simplest way is often the best. What would happen if every ministry of the church began to give some of its efforts to an outside-church experience? For example, what if the Trustees Work Day at church also included an hour of picking up trash in the surrounding neighborhood and, even better, flyers had been sent out inviting the neighbors to get involved and to partake in a light "thank you" meal afterward? What if the choir placed an ad in the local paper inviting people outside the church to join the choir in preparing special music presentations for Christmas or Easter? What if the choir shared its cantata that they spent three months preparing by performing at local nursing homes or community shelters or even the mall? What if . . . ? Once the inside-church groups begin to think of ways to become involved with the community outside the church, the possibilities expand, and in the process the church begins to develop a mind-set that the whole community is the place of God's caring and sharing. Consider these suggestions:

■ Do VBS in a community center, instead of the church, in cooperation with other community groups that care about kids. Some folks would like for their children to have the experience but get nervous coming into a church building.

■ Have a women's group work with the local hospital to host a women's safety and health day.

■ Have a men's group offer to rebuild and repair small maintenance items for elderly neighbors near the church and invite men from the community to get involved.

These things would not be done to make the church look good. They would be done because the church is good and wants to reflect God's compassion to others.

As teams form naturally, that is the time to reinforce the missional skills of building teams that are Christ-centered; teaching the team to be intentional about engaging in conversation with people outside the church and listening with care; keeping their eyes open to the constant possibility of a new partner in the work, maybe someone they would never have thought of before; and constantly connecting with God in prayer, asking, "How can we fit in with your will now?"

The potential for multiplying mission teams is exponential. As more and more people experience the joy of being involved in demonstrating God's goodness in partnership with a hurting world, they become aware of their ability to connect with the greater whole. This is the kingdom of God among us—no part or person unimportant, no part or person overlooked, and no part or person too small to be involved. Before you know it, your church will be increasingly engaged with the community, and their excitement about being used by God to demonstrate the gospel of Jesus Christ will become infectious. Your church will have moved through the change process from event, to trend, to a change in heart and mind. The next stage in the change process is changing the structures of the church to be more effective in God's mission. Such change can be a daunting and dangerous task; however, the process so far has set the stage to lay the groundwork for positive change—a process we will turn our attention to in the next chapter.

"The vision was to involve as many people from the community as possible. Businesses as well as individuals joined with us. It is a real blessing to actually do God's work beyond the church walls, rather than merely talking about it."
—Mill Creek Baptist Church, Leroy, WV

Key Points

■ It's important to understand that God is not waiting on us to do God's restoration mission. If we won't play, others will. God has proved this over and over again, even as Jesus chose "tax collectors and sinners" rather than religious leaders to reveal God's power.

■ When something new stretches us, the change force must continue or else we snap back to our previous condition. The likelihood of sustained growth increases by realizing that, while all change starts with a single event, that event must multiply and grow into a trend for change to continue.

■ To get from an event to a trend, one experience with community engagement must expand into more. As more and more people experience the joy of being involved in demonstrating God's goodness in partnership with a hurting world, they become aware of their ability to connect with the greater whole.

■ It is important not to waste effort on reorganizing church structures before the hearts and minds of the church members are prepared by a wide acceptance of missional experience and reflection.

■ The very act of listening will itself have impact on your community and your church. Imagine a church that cares enough about people to ask for their opinion. The church that learns to listen for the passion expressed by people both inside and outside the church will find the source of limitless energy for ministry.

CHAPTER 6

Change Skills and Dancing with Danger

As the saying goes, "Nobody likes change except a wet baby!" As we start this last technology session, we acknowledge that if a church begins to multiply mission teams, the very nature of the church is going to change. In close-knit church communities many members (and pastors) fear upsetting members with the effects of change, and thus they maintain a "business as usual," status quo ministry of the church. So how do we navigate the inevitable change that comes to a church as it becomes more missional? While this topic is too big and too individualized for an in-depth study during the MCLE process, it is also too important not to discuss the reality and to prepare the participants with a few simple skills to help them keep change as positive as possible.

We start the session by asking the group, "How might your church be different five years from now, if mission teams multiplied and became a major focus of your church's ministry?" The responses are interesting to hear, and participants usually fall into two categories: (1) the visionaries, who see a bright future with excited Christians gathering on Sunday brimming with stories of seeing God at work that week in their community involvement, and (2) the realists, who with somber faces and anxious body language express that they know what will happen if mission teams abound in their church—there will be war.

In practice, both responses most commonly happen simultaneously. As mission teams multiply, some people in the church will be energized by having their faith come alive through community engagement, and some will want nothing to do with these efforts and wish things would just go back to the way they were. The next question usually helps the teams find their focus: "What will happen to your church in five years if it does not get outside the walls of the church and care about the community?" It is evident from their reactions that this question helps them realize what is at stake, and that awareness begins to help them put aside the fear of conflict.

On a personal note, I am very aware as I go through this process with churches that many of them will taste the missional church movement, see that it is good, but choose not to continue toward becoming more missional. I accept this reality and believe that it is still important to give churches experience with the missional movement so they can make an informed choice. But I also hope and pray that even in those churches who do not continue to develop an outward focus for their church ministry, enough seeds will be planted to help individual Christians get involved and stay involved with God's restorative mission all the days of their lives. Planting seeds is important, as is believing that the harvest is in the hands of God, who is living in a future we cannot fully comprehend.

Introduction to Change Skills

At this point in the session, I use the analogy of marriage preparation. I explain how, as a pastor, I try to prepare young couples for marriage by telling them that even if they have a healthy, strong marriage, they will likely experience at least two or three crises during which they might feel that their marriage is in danger of failing. If they recognize that these times are common and refuse to panic, they will be able to seize the opportunity to grow toward a better future, one where their marriage not only survives, but thrives. This is what God is offering churches—not simply a chance to survive change, but to thrive in the midst of it, allowing change to take us into the deep places of God. These can be wonderful times of opportunity for the church to readjust our relationships. The key is to *not panic*, to stay in the process and find new life and purpose that lead to the richness of weathering the storm together. It also helps to recognize that many people resist change because they are simply overwhelmed with other changes in their lives, and they need the church to provide a place of stability. So as your church navigates the tsunami of change, remember: resistance to change is normal, don't panic, trust God, and look for the opportunities. Your church can begin laying the groundwork for positive change by teaching two important values: (1) covenant relationships and (2) respect for one another's call.

Covenant Communities

We live in a contract world, and all contracts are based upon performance. As a simple example, let's say that I will sell you my lawnmower for $50. If you provide the $50, you get the lawnmower; no $50, no lawnmower. The problem comes when we apply this contract mentality to our relationships. We were created to be a covenant people in relationship with God and one another. In a covenant relationship, each party promises to do what is right and best for the other, and each party is responsible for keeping their promise regardless of the other party's performance. Everyone

"There is starting to be some buzz about becoming missional. I am excited about future shifts in our approach to ministry!"
—Rev. Dr. Anthony G. Pappas, Executive Minister, American Baptist Churches of Massachusetts

does their own work of trying to be true to their word without consuming themselves with another's response. God through Christ demonstrated the restoration of our covenant relationship with God, and God keeps this promise to us. Having received God's love and forgiveness and being empowered by God's Spirit, we are now invited to live in like manner toward others: forgiving their sins against us and repaying evil with good. The gospel may be simple, but it is never easy. In teaching this value, I hope that members of a church can begin to see the importance of living in a covenant community where they are bound to one another's well-being as citizens of God's domain. This is God's kingdom model to the world. Building on this covenant relationship, the church can agree that we are in this change together, and together we will work out our issues related to change.

Respect Each Call

The second value, respect for one another's call, leaves room for everyone to discern their part in the covenant community with the good of the community in mind. For years seminaries have taught Pareto's Principle, which is that 20 percent of the people do 80 percent of the work.[1] Churches put a great deal of effort into trying to convince the 80 percent that they really need to do more of their share of the work, yet their words seem to fall on deaf ears. The missional movement asks some interesting questions: What if by God's design only 20 percent of the people are called to the inner workings of the church? What if it only requires roughly 20 percent of the Christians to do the necessary organizing and care for worship, facilities, music, etc.? What if the purpose of the 20 percent were to create the support necessary for the 80 percent to receive inspiring worship, training for ministry, and nurturing so that the 80 percent can be equipped to go outside the church and become involved with God in God's restorative mission with the world?

Those of us who have a call to the church's inner work (i.e., worship, leadership, etc.) have a tendency to believe everyone should be like us, but they are not. Perhaps the reason we can never compel the 80 percent to participate in the church's inner life is because it simply was not their call to begin with, and rather we are failing to acknowledge that others are called to service outside the walls of the church, with God, in the world. Time and again, MCLE teams have told how the marginal people in their church, those who had never volunteered for anything before, got involved in their mission team.

With these two values affirmed—covenant commitment to the church and respect for each other's call—the church can create processes that allow conversations to happen for supporting change. Some churches hold an annual Vision Sunday, or offer regular listening sessions. Many models for church communication are available. The important point is to have a regular opportunity for persons who are invested in the ministry to share their thoughts and concerns and to respectfully listen to one another. Also, it is important to create occasional opportunities for recommitment to one another in both God's work among us and God's work through us to others. These intentional conversations inform church leadership and help the church determine ways to build bridges between different groups in the church who may experience God's call in different modes. Once people see each other as

"The MCLE process has been creating some very positive thinking among the people in the congregation. People who are not on the committee are actually getting involved in projects that the committee has not initiated!"
—Rev. Dr. Louise Barger, First Baptist Church of Greater Des Moines, Des Moines, IA

part of the whole, they experience their own participation as necessary and valued. Whatever process is used for these important conversations about change, they need to be repeated as often as necessary to keep the dialogue open in the church.

The Role of the Local Congregation in the Missional Movement

During this discussion church teams are asked, "What changes might come to your church as it becomes more missional?" This question takes a good bit of imagination since most of the participants have yet to experience a fully functioning missional church, but their answers generally fall into three categories: worship that inspires, equipping for ministry, and nurturing support for Christians as they live out the gospel in their community.

Worship That Inspires

Helping people capture a vision for God's restoration in the new heaven and the new earth builds an imperative for involvement in the world now. Worship helps establish the critical link between the missional movement and the Lord's Prayer, which states, "Your kingdom come, your will be done, on earth as it is in heaven" (Matthew 6:10). Music, art forms, and messages that help people comprehend the restorative mission of God and conceptualize the promised outcome are all important.

Worship can also help reform our thinking from salvation as "fire insurance," providing heaven someday, to salvation today, living as citizens of God's reality now. Through worship we are invited to join God in expressing the Good News in every aspect of life. Worship becomes joyful, visionary, and hopeful and has the effect of empowering people to be part of God's goodness now, to participate in something bigger than they are. It moves worship away from the expression of merely a personal relationship with God to the more comprehensive, corporate understanding that we are already a part of a whole new creation that is being fulfilled by the resurrection power of God. We become a people who believe that God keeps promises, and that God is willing and able to show us how we can participate fully in living this new reality. Missional worship can be expressed in any style; it is being part of the missional God that forms its heartbeat.

Equipping for Ministry

As Christians get involved in living their whole lives as God's mission agents, demonstrating the Good News of God and the restoration, they will become increasingly aware of what they need to be effective. Christian education will shift from the traditional classroom educational model to providing skills for ministry in motion. Some of the equipping will be practical, such as leadership skills to form and direct mission teams, conflict-transformation skills for handling disputes that arise during community work, discipleship skills for people who express an interest in Christianity during community work, and sociology and counseling skills to be effective in understanding and meeting the needs they encounter in the community. Other equipping skills will be spiritual, such as how to balance personal development and ministry opportunities, tools for staying connected to Christ as the source of life, and developing Christian character under the demands of human involvement.

The MCLE itself is designed to offer a model of equipping Christians for the work of the ministry through an action/reflection

"After nearly forty years of activities inside the church, the MCLE showed us how to take the church out into the community, where it really belongs."
—Cornerstone Baptist Church, Danielson, CT

process that happens within a small team that reports to a larger community. The MCLE encourages people to form small groups that jump into ministry involvement and "learn by doing." While engaged in action the participants are taught to ask questions, discover lessons, and uncover needs for more training. The team then participates in a learning community that gives the disciples a safe place to debrief their experience with similarly committed Christians. As individuals share what they have learned from their experience, others also learn. The support from the group fosters accountability to keep the participants involved in missional efforts and helps them maintain their focus on Christ. With the increased use of the Internet, future ministry-equipping efforts will most certainly include resources accessed through virtual communities where people will share ministry experiences and exchange best practices. This offers the advantage of connecting local efforts with larger segments of Christians and learning from an ever-increasing pool of contributors.

Nurturing Support for Christians as Ministers

Ministry is hard work. As the world gets more complex, so do the demands of working with people. As more Christians move from sitting in pews to engaging outside the church walls, the church has an opportunity to respond by offering care and nurture to the Christian servants to help them remain fruitful in the work. Think of missionaries in foreign cultures who need a place to rest, reflect, and regroup before moving back into service. So too, today's Christians will need a safe place to retreat for periods of renewal, reflection, and companionship with those who understand their passion and involvement with God's mission with the world. They will need a sanctuary with Christians who are ready to help heal their fatigue and regenerate their strength for the next effort.

In Luke 9:1-6, 10-17, we see Jesus use this model of discipleship when he sent out the Twelve to learn by engaging in ministry.

When they returned he received them unto himself, listened to them recount their stories, celebrated their experiences, and offered important points of instruction. Then he called them to simple acts of rest such as retreating from the hectic environment and sharing a meal, all in preparation for further service. There are Christians who have the gift of hospitality and nurture to help with this important work. Some have the gift of giving counsel through listening and helping people reflect on their experiences. Still others have the gift of creating sacred spaces for rest and refreshment, and others have worship gifts that draw us into the healing presence of God. What a glorious purpose for the church when those gifts are being used to help mend and mold more ministers to work with God in the field ripe for harvest.

As the traditional church becomes more outwardly focused there will be periods of stress and stretching that will require strong, positive leadership that can call the community together to respect and love one another even as the systems change. This is not the first challenge the church has faced, and there will certainly be many more to come. It takes faith—"confidence in what we hope for and assurance about what we do not see" (Hebrews 11:1)—to navigate through this seismic challenge. For many pastors this means serving as pastor of two churches: the ones who cannot change, and the ones who cannot wait to get started on the future. Many of today's pastors are just the right people for the job. It is as though they were born for this time of transition. To all those pastors, I salute you for your courage, faith, and perseverance.

"Our involvement with the community has helped our church work together as a team. The greatest lesson learned is that hard work is necessary, and it takes a team to do ministry of this kind."
—Mt. Pleasant Baptist Church, Providence, RI

Key Points

■ In close-knit church communities many members (and pastors) fear upsetting members with the effects of change, and thus they maintain a "business as usual," status quo ministry of the church.

■ God is offering churches not simply a chance to survive change, but to thrive in the midst of it, allowing change to take us into the deep places of God.

■ Helping people capture a vision for God's restoration in the new heaven and the new earth builds an imperative for involvement in the world now.

■ The missional movement asks: What if by God's design only 20 percent of the people are called to the inner workings of the church? What if the purpose of the 20 percent were to create the support necessary for the 80 percent to receive inspiring worship, training for ministry, and nurturing so that the 80 percent can be equipped to go outside the church and become involved with God in God's restorative mission with the world?

■ As the traditional church becomes more outwardly focused there will be periods of stress and stretching that will require strong, positive leadership that can call the community together to respect and love one another even as the systems change.

Note

1. F. John Reh, "Pareto's Principle—The 80-20 Rule," management.about.com/cs/generalmanagement/a/Pareto08 1202.htm, accessed August 4, 2012.

CHAPTER 7

Session 3 — Telling God's Story

After months of preparation Session 3 arrives—the day when teams tell stories about the lessons learned through their involvement with their communities in God's restorative mission. Stories are very important. Many of the Bible's greatest truths are taught through stories. After opening worship, we start with a reminder that our stories are extensions of God's story, using the story of The Widow's Offering (Luke 21:1-4) as our example. The widow represented several groups of marginalized people: women, the elderly, and the poor. No one but Jesus noticed her gift at the temple treasury. By telling her story, Jesus ensured that her story would be remembered and later added to the Bible. Throughout the last two millennia wherever the story of Jesus has been told, so too has been the story of The Widow's Offering. If we could see all the funds raised and good accomplished through the telling of her story, we would be stunned. When God tells our story amazing results can happen, no matter how small our offering seems to us. So our stories are not ours alone, but rather are meant to be shared for the benefit of others.

Learning from One Another's Stories

Prior to Session 3 the churches have been coached to prepare a five-to seven-minute presentation of what they have learned about themselves, God, and the mission through their community involvement. When making their presentations, they are encouraged to be as creative as their imaginations will allow. Some churches have set their stories to music. First Baptist Church of Oelwein, Iowa, sang their story to the tune of the theme song from *The Beverly Hillbillies*, and First Baptist Church of Cuba, New York, rewrote the words to "Jesus Loves the Little Children." Some teams have created comedy skits that would rival those by the best professional comedians. First Baptist Church of Berkeley, California, created a comedic skit entitled "To, For, or With" about the missional quality of involving everyone in the mission. Others have PowerPoint presentations with pictures and graphics. Wakefield Baptist Church (Rhode Island) designed a drama complete with masks that displayed their different emotions as they went through the process. Phenix Baptist Church (Rhode Island) used a children's table and chairs to represent how their team felt like children as they worked to find a way to become involved with their community. San Leandro Community Church, California, designed a *Jeopardy!*-style MCLE Game that had the whole room rolling with laughter.

The teams are also reminded that the purpose of sharing our stories within the learning community is to learn from one another, and that we often learn more from our struggles than from our victories. So while good-news stories are told with delight, we also fully enter into the very real stories of frustration and disappointment. The very nature of experiments includes the possibility that they may fail. All the stories earnestly reflect the teams' efforts to become involved with God in the world around us. After each presentation, the learning community breaks into small groups to discuss what they learned about being missional from the presenting team's story. While each story is unique and important, some common lessons have emerged from the many encounters. These lessons are illustrated in the following stories.

Partners Multiply Effectiveness

Until recently, the children of one inner-city Indianapolis neighborhood had only a 20-by-20-foot grassy space in which to play—just outside Rev. Tom Jackson's office window at Tuxedo Park Baptist Church. Participating in the MCLE, the church expanded the outdoor play area by obtaining from the city abandoned properties located just across the street from the church.

"It's the only place for the children to meet. They're out here every day with soccer balls and baseballs—Haitian children whose mothers and fathers are Muslim, Hispanic kids, Caucasian kids, and African American kids," comments Pastor Jackson. "They don't always speak the same language, but a soccer ball transcends that. We have an opportunity to minister to these kids and their moms and dads."

The city demolished four buildings on the properties whose facades had collapsed, creating additional open space of approximately 100 by 200 feet. On April 30, 2011, approximately 125 volunteers from the Tuxedo Park church, three other churches, and the community gathered to clean and prepare the area for the children's use.

Since the church is located in one of the highest-crime neighborhoods in Indianapolis, it received a $10,000 grant from the 2012 Indianapolis Super Bowl Host Committee's Legacy Project, which helped to revitalize the city as part of its preparations for hosting Super Bowl XLVI. In addition, the nonprofit organization

"It is hard to believe we have almost completed our learning time together! I hope and pray some other churches will get on board for another MCLE in Michigan. This journey has been *most* valuable!"
—Rev. Gretchen Sanewsky, First Baptist Church, Jackson, MI

Keep Indianapolis Beautiful provided funds for project materials and leadership.

Pastor Jackson recounted a visit from an affluent man who marveled that the children felt safe to play in the church's space despite the neighborhood's high crime rate. "As he watched the children playing, I asked him how many of the parents from his community would let their children play outside in such a high crime area. His answer was, 'None of them.'" Pastor Jackson replied, "Here, at Tuxedo Park Baptist Church, Christ has given us all a beautiful mission opportunity that we celebrate."[1]

One Opportunity Leads to Others

In a place where winter temperatures can dip below zero, it's difficult to imagine that senior citizens in Maine look forward to the season. However, throughout the year in Farmington, many seniors and people with disabilities eagerly await January's arrival because of the camaraderie, prayer, and hot meals provided at a warming center that resulted from Henderson Memorial Baptist Church's participation in the MCLE.

"The Warming Center was wildly successful from the start. A genuine community of guests developed over the first winter," states Rev. Dr. Susan Crane, pastor of Henderson Memorial. "Come the Fourth of July, many of the regulars showed up on our church lawn to watch the parade. One after another told me they couldn't wait for winter to come again."

When Henderson Memorial was invited to participate in one of the first MCLE learning communities it was suffering from poor morale, the result of an earlier church split. In addition, the aging church was hurting financially. Approximately half of the church's ninety-six members were over the age of seventy, and the 1940s structure was difficult to heat. With heating oil at $4.50 per gallon in 2008, the church could only open for Sunday worship, keeping the thermostat at a meager 56 degrees all other times.

Yet when Henderson Memorial attended the MCLE, it met the challenge of becoming active outside its own walls. Using the MCLE process, the church team asked the community for their input and responded when the Franklin County Emergency Management director expressed fear that citizens might freeze in their homes because they couldn't afford the cost of heating oil. The church couldn't finance the warming center alone and enlisted the help of two other churches. The Warming Center debuted in 2009, open from January through March, with the three churches rotating as host. Approximately forty lunches are served daily, provided by another of their partners, Seniors Plus, part of the Area Agency on Aging that serves western Maine. However, people of all ages do attend as well as volunteer.

"People enjoy gathering for conversation before lunch and like to stay after to work on activities and crafts," says Pastor Crane. "But the thing they all buzz about as our third season approaches is that, at the Warming Center, we can *pray*, as we do before the meal, and also read inspirational stories, which often spark pastoral conversations that encourage people to minister to each other."

In April 2010 the governor asked Pastor Crane to present a workshop at the Maine State Emergency Management Agency's convention, helping other churches and organizations learn from their efforts how to help their own communities. That led to creating a

"At a time when retirement has become an option, the missional focus has captured my interest and my heart and I'm anxious to see what else we can do in missional ways to expand the Lord's work here in the Cuba area."
—Rev. Larry Poelma, Cuba First Baptist Church, Cuba, NY

guide on founding and running a warming center for the United Way of the Tri-Valley Area.[2]

New Generations Forming a Missional Focus

During Session 1 of his MCLE learning community in Iowa, Rev. Joshua Meyer, Pastor of Discipleship at First Baptist Church, Clinton, was particularly captured by the challenge to find out how many young adults in his town were actively engaged with a Christian church. When he finished gathering the data he was staggered to learn that only 4 percent of people under forty were attending church in his town. Using the MCLE process, Pastor Meyer began to imagine a new generation of church where everyone was involved in some sort of community improvement and the church served to inspire, train, and nurture their involvement. As a result "The Cause" was born in 2011, a church based on the Matthew 25:31-46 passage where the people of God are those who serve others.

Pastor Meyer explains, "The Cause has given us an opportunity to train young and old alike to strive to be authentic in their Christian faith. They are hungering for more support, accountability, and training. Excitement and expectation are emerging as they are called to service, rather than just church attendance. There is a desire to learn more about how Jesus taught us to serve others, and people are beginning to recognize community needs such as poverty, addiction, abuse, and neglect. Fervor for prayer is coming forth as people are praying for these experiences to be more than outreach, but an opportunity to do ministry *with* people instead of just *to* people. Ultimately, people are excited to put their faith into action and become the hands and feet of Jesus with their community."

Numerous projects have resulted so far, and no project is too big or too small to be considered. People have shoveled snow after a 16-inch storm. One group is delivering meals while another is delivering clothes. Others are joining local organizations like Big Brothers Big Sisters or organizing rides to church. All activities are connected to their total life experience of living the gospel of Jesus Christ.

"Many people are faithfully answering the call to be part of something bigger than they are, as well as larger than their previous thoughts about church," states Pastor Meyer. "A change is taking root as they recognize that they can be a part of The Cause of Jesus Christ."[3]

Small Churches Can Have Big Impact

The MCLE missional project for Send the Light Community Fellowship was to reach the approximately seventy-five students who rode the late buses to and from Frankfort Elementary School, kindergarten through fifth grade, with a healthy snack for their weekends at home. These students came from the poorest portion of northern Greenbrier County, WV, and for many the only real food they got was the breakfast and lunch served on school days. On Fridays from January through the end of the school year in June, each student received a bag filled with healthy snacks and juice boxes to take home for the weekend.

Since the entire membership of the church was seven adults, everyone was involved. One couple took on the mission of buying the food from local warehouses, while others went to community

"We have a new understanding of what our ministry is all about since we entered the MCLE. We have learned that it is not about us; our faith gives us the power to make the world a better place. We began looking at everything that we do through the lens of being a missional church."

—First Baptist Church, Norwich, CT

organizations to raise funds to match the $1,000 "seed" grant given by the American Baptist Home Mission Societies for the effort. During the church's Saturday evening meetings, another couple organized the process of making up the snack packs. One member was also a teacher at the school and was able to get the necessary approvals. The group learned to work with the system by distributing the bags only after school because county policies restricted children from receiving food from outside sources during the school day. The church was even allowed to include a "love note" in each bag that said, "This Love in a Brown Bag is given to you from Send the Light Community Fellowship, a home church community of believers in Jesus Christ whose mission is to Love God, Love Others, and Serve the World. Enjoy the food and have a wonderful weekend!"

It did not take long for the church to learn that God's plans are greater than we can imagine. While their original plan was to give food bags from January until Easter break, God called others to become generously involved, providing more than double the original $1,000 grant and making distributions possible through the end of the school year. There was even enough food left over to give to a local shelter for abused women and children.

"We live in a very rural area and have few businesses, but we were amazed to see local churches, civic organizations, and individuals come on board to help us financially," reported Rev. Jim Anderson, president of the fellowship. "We were deeply moved by the gratitude of the children, and when they asked if we were going to keep on giving out food every Friday, we felt joy—but also heartbreak as we saw firsthand some of the sad situations our teachers see every day.

"Because of this involvement, we realized that our Lord has a purpose for our fellowship outside of our homes, and in September we applied for and received IRS 501(c) church status so we can now apply for grants from other sources to continue our missional approach to the Frankfort community and school."

The team reported there were times when the MCLE process felt difficult, but they were encouraged by their MCLE local coordinator and facilitator to keep on track. Pastor Anderson concluded, "We praise God for the opportunity not only to be missional, but also to experience the excitement of other churches as they went beyond their comfort zones to reach out with the love of Jesus."[4]

Finishing Well

Following the presentations and the group's discussion about the lessons learned, the learning community takes a few minutes to review the main missional principles and action steps used throughout the MCLE process. This review is intended to help the participants finish with a holistic understanding of what they have been doing in small steps, and includes the following recommendations for developing future mission teams.

■ Create a church culture that encourages people to recognize that their passions and interest in making the community better are part of their total Christian life.

■ Form mission teams to explore possible involvement with the community.

■ Follow the four-step process taught in the MCLE:

■ Step 1—Building Our Mission Team: Discipleship Central: have every mission team be intentional about creating a Christian community among themselves, which can be shared with others who join their efforts, and ask every team to communicate with the church as they go through their steps of community involvement.

"Our greatest lesson learned is the sense of community we now all feel."
—Webster Baptist Church, Webster, NY

■ Step 2—Learning to Listen to Our Community: send the mission teams out to hear what is on the hearts and minds of the community before deciding what action to take.

■ Step 3—Looking for Potential Mission Partners in Our Community: see what God is already doing; have the mission teams look for those who are already active in the area and learn what they are doing that might offer potential ministry partnerships.

■ Step 4—Discerning Our Part in God's Mission: have the mission teams review the information gathered in Step 2 and Step 3 and pray for direction, then have them develop a written plan of action that answers the "who, what, where, when, how" questions.

It has become tradition for learning communities to conclude their MCLE with a service of Communion hosted by the local coordinator. Each group expresses this in a different style, but the effect is to thank God and one another for investing in this experimental exploration of the future of Christianity in the U.S. We usually remind ourselves of the opening line from Session 1: "Congratulations, you have been chosen to serve the Lord during the most accelerated rate of change in human experience." During this time people often reflect on the changes that have occurred over the year that the learning community has been meeting as a sample of this astounding truth. We then reflect on another statement from Session 1: "God has placed you in this time to be transition agents from a Christian heritage that we knew and understood to a future that we cannot even imagine." We consider the questions: What can we take forward? What will need to be left behind as we pass the baton of faith to future generations?

Beyond MCLE

The imagery of the Lord's Supper becomes very clear as we share it in the closing session of the MCLE. The disciples entered that upper room as students of the Teacher. They had experienced some amazing events. Yet they remained in the student role with the Teacher bearing most of the responsibility. As that night unfolded it became clear that the Teacher was now appointing them to become apostles, meaning "sent ones," to shift from being the student to becoming the teacher for others. They did not feel ready, as the story attests. However, Jesus knew the only way they would continue to grow into full spiritual maturity was for them to take responsibility for the growth of others.

So it is as we conclude the MCLE. This is only the beginning of our exploration of faith in the future; our growth will continue as we continue to grasp the full delivery of the gospel with words and deeds, delivered in loving relationships. The next step for the mission teams is becoming teachers for others as they share what they are learning. The group is encouraged to consider the following actions to keep the momentum of becoming learners and teachers of missional church:

■ Write your story of community involvement and send it to the MCLE facilitator for use across the country to help other churches learn from your experience and follow you into God's mission.

■ Contact your local coordinator and express an interest in forming an alumni group that stays connected for continuing education opportunities on a semiannual or annual basis.

■ Attend another MCLE by bringing another team from your church through the process.

■ Serve as part of the support team for another MCLE learning community. (An invitation is sent when a new learning community is developing in your area. Previous participants are invited to support the new learning community by attending sessions, sitting with church teams, hearing their discussions, offering personal experiences, and sharing in support efforts of the local coordinator and MCLE facilitator.)

■ Participate in follow-up opportunities such as webinars. (Invitations are sent as available.)

■ Form your own MCLE learning community with churches in your area, using resources offered by the sponsoring partner, American Baptist Home Mission Societies (www.abhms.org), this book and the companion *Facilitator's Guide*, available from Judson Press (www.judsonpress.com). The MCLE facilitator also provides a list of other resources available through the American Baptist Home Mission Societies to aid in missional efforts.

Benediction: "Hallowed Be Your Name"

While on a plane trip recently, I found myself reading the very familiar Lord's Prayer when something new caught my attention. For the first time I noticed the connection between the line "Hallowed be your name" and the next line, "Your kingdom come, your will be done, on earth as it is in heaven." I found myself asking, is there a connection between these two ideas? Will God's peaceable reign come upon the earth when God's name is held in high esteem? And what would it take to cause God to be revered? Suddenly, I had a thought and began flipping through my Bible to confirm it. I found that every time Jesus did something good—cured a leper, restored sight, fed the people—the very next statement in the Bible is, "And the people praised God!" I had never noticed that before. It implies that seeing acts of remarkable goodness caused the people to honor God. Then a thought occurred to me: is that what the missional movement is all about—allowing people to see Christians doing good and so begin to praise God? And if the people begin to praise God, will it increase God's reign of peace upon the earth? I'll let you decide.

Key Points

■ The very nature of experiments includes the possibility that they may fail.

■ The purpose of sharing our stories within the learning community is to learn from one another, and we often learn more from our struggles than from our victories.

■ God's plans are greater than we can imagine.

■ Jesus knew the only way his disciples would continue to grow into full spiritual maturity was for them to take responsibility for the growth of others. Our growth will continue as we continue to grasp the full delivery of the gospel with words and deeds, delivered in loving relationships.

■ The missional movement allows people to see Christians reflecting God's goodness and may lead to others praising God.

Congratulations—you have been chosen to serve the Lord during the most accelerated rate of change in human experience.

Notes

1. Nadine Hasenecz, "Church expands outdoor play area for inner-city children," May 2011, www.abhms.org/front_center_tuxedo_park_church_outdr_ply2011.cfm, accessed June 21, 2012.

2. Nadine Hasenecz, "MCLE-inspired warming center melts frozen Farmington winters," January 2011, www.abhms.org/front_center_henderson_memorial_2011.cfm, accessed June 21, 2012.

3. Joshua Meyer, "MCLE leads Iowa church to 'The Cause,'" May 2011, www.abhms.org/mcle/fbc_clinton_the_cause.cfm, accessed June 21, 2012.

4. Jim Anderson, "Love in a Brown Bag," *The Christian Citizen*, 1 (2010): 9.

APPENDICES

APPENDIX A

Missional Church Learning Experience Guidelines

The Missional Church Learning Experience (MCLE) materials were originally developed by American Baptist Home Mission Societies (National Ministries) and made possible by faithful contributions to the America for Christ offering and generous United Mission gifts. Permission to photocopy, adapt, or otherwise reproduce these materials is granted to the purchaser for congregational use only with the following credit line: Adapted from Glynis LaBarre, *Learning Mission, Living Mission: Churches That Work* in "Living Church," J. Dwight Stinnett, series ed. (Valley Forge, PA: Judson Press, 2012). Copyright © 2012 by Judson Press. Used by permission of the publisher. www.judsonpress.com.

Missional Church Learning Experience Guidelines
In Partnership with [ORGANIZATION NAME AS APPROPRIATE]

Thank you for your interest in the Missional Church Learning Experience (MCLE). These guidelines are intended to help you determine if this opportunity would benefit your efforts in effective church ministry. Please consider the information and contact [NAME] at [ORGANIZATION / EMAIL / PHONE] to ask questions or discuss details.

Missional Church Learning Experience Overview
Churches throughout the United States are looking for ways to bring vitality to their ministries. Currently there is a lot of talk about the missional church movement, but ideas need to be practiced to become effective. The Missional Church Learning Experience is designed to introduce churches to the missional church movement through a practical, "hands-on" learning experience in partnership with other church teams in the form of a learning community.

This mission focus for the church is based on the belief that God created the church body to deliver the Good News for humanity through communities of faith that display God's love among themselves as they work to deliver Christ's message of God's love to the world. When a church is "on mission" with God they are demonstrating the gospel as Christ did: through word and deed, delivered in loving relationships empowered by God's Spirit. Christians strengthen one another for this work by forming Christian communities (local churches) that inspire through worship, train for effective mission, and support disciples to serve as God's life-giving agents.

When a local church forgets God's purpose for the church body, it can become a self-serving entity. Refocusing outward on God's mission in their community helps Christians regain their purpose, bringing life and vitality to the church. As Christians become engaged with people in their community in caring ways, their own discipleship improves and the community sees *Christianity that works—faith that makes a difference*, to everyone's advantage.

You Are Invited . . .

If your association of churches would like to form a Missional Church Learning Experience in partnership with [FACILIATATOR AND/OR ORGANIZATION NAME], together we will:

■ create a learning community of mission teams from six to twelve churches

■ introduce basic missional principles in an eight-month period through three sessions in person and four technology training sessions (one hour for each technology session)

■ help the church teams design and implement a small, interactive community involvement that practices missional principles

■ equip the church teams with healthy, repeatable patterns to multiply missional efforts

■ share what is learned with the learning community and other churches for continued growth in missional qualities

Association of Churches' Responsibilities:

■ Express a desire to participate in a MCLE, Missional Church Learning Experience, by contacting [NAME /ORGANIZATION], and schedule a review of the MCLE Guidelines.

■ Provide a coordinator (may be a volunteer, lay or clergy) to work with the MCLE facilitator to implement the MCLE in the following ways:

■ Complete the MCLE Request form, signed by a representative of the requesting association of churches.

■ Recruit six to twelve churches to participate in a learning community, making every effort to *encourage diverse ethnic participation* (Addendum A).

■ Make host and worship arrangements for the three MCLE in-person sessions for the learning community over an eight-month period.

■ Provide support for the learning community between training sessions, with assistance from the MCLE facilitator.

■ Participate in the Coordinators' Advisory Council (CAC), an advisory group composed of all MCLE coordinators, through conference calls and occasional other opportunities to help improve the MCLE process.

■ Share what is learned through the experience with others in the association of churches.

Participating Churches' Responsibilities:

■ Accept the invitation to participate in a MCLE learning community by signing the MCLE Covenant Agreement (Addendum A) and returning it to the local coordinator.

■ Gather a mission team of five participants for the eight-month period (Addendum A).

■ Participate in the three in-person sessions and four technology training sessions of the MCLE learning community.

■ Complete the four-step process to practice healthy, repeatable patterns for community ministry.

■ Design and implement a small community involvement to practice missional principles, investing church resources of time, money, and energy in community partnerships.

■ Share what is learned through the experience with others in the learning community and with the association of churches.

MCLE Facilitator's Responsibilities:

■ Review the MCLE Guidelines with representatives of the church association, and work with the designated coordinator to review the Learning Agreement (Addendum B) and MCLE Request.

■ Provide the coordinator with MCLE materials to help establish a MCLE learning community.

■ Implement the MCLE process, in cooperation with the coordinator, over the eight-month period, including the three in-person sessions and four technology sessions.

■ Support the learning community between sessions, with the coordinator's assistance.

■ Share with other churches what participating churches have learned, for the good of all.

■ Issue "Certificates of Completion" to churches that finish the MCLE process.

Missional Church Learning Experience
Proposed Timeline

Pre-Launch (1–3 months)	**Church association expresses interest in forming a MCLE learning community:** ■ Review MCLE Guidelines with MCLE facilitator ■ Select local coordinator .■ Return the completed MCLE Request ■ Select dates for all MCLE sessions ■ Invite participating churches using MCLE materials ■ Have churches select their mission team members ■ Plan Session 1
Months 1–4	**Session 1— "Getting Started on the Future"** ■ Worship ■ Our current reality ■ Introduction to the missional church movement ■ Overview of MCLE process ■ Learning Community Covenant Technology session #1: "First Steps Into Mission" (one hour) ■ Step 1—"Building Our Mission Team: Discipleship Central" ■ Step 2—"Learning to Listen to Our Community" Technology session #2: "Steps for Growing More Missional" (one hour) ■ Step 3—"Looking for Potential Mission Partners in Our Community" ■ Step 4—"Discerning Our Part in God's Mission"

Months
5–8

Session 2—"Building Healthy, Repeatable Patterns"
■ Worship
■ Results of four-step process for community ministry
■ Presentation of community project ideas
■ Application of missional principles to refine community project plans
■ Learning community's commitment to engagement
Technology session #3: "Multiplying Missional Efforts" (one hour)
Technology session #4: "Change Skills" (one hour)

Session 3—"Telling God's Story"
■ Worship
■ Presentation of teams' experiences with community
■ Lessons learned
■ Resources for next steps
■ Celebration of God's mission

Beyond . . .

Recognition and Follow-up
■ Collect one-page stories from churches to be shared with others
■ Issue "Certificates of Completion" to church teams that finish the process
■ Gather church assessments of the experience
■ Develop alumni group plans

Addendum A
Your Church Is Invited to Participate in a
Missional Church Learning Experience
Church Covenant and Application

Your church is invited to participate in an eight-month experience designed to introduce congregations to the missional church movement to help them become more effective in demonstrating Christ's love within their communities. Your church will be part of a learning community of churches that receives three in-person training sessions supplemented by four technology sessions. You will practice the missional principles using a four-step process to help you design and implement a small community engagement to practice healthy, repeatable patterns for further community ministry. You will share your experience with other church teams in the MCLE learning community.

This covenant represents mutual commitments by your local church, your local association of churches (<u>NAME</u>), and facilitator (<u>NAME</u>) toward the pursuit of a missional church ministry emphasis. Together with God's leading we can attain the goal of increasingly effective ministry.

The Association of Churches (<u>name</u>) agrees to:

1. Provide a local coordinator to work with the MCLE facilitator toward an effective learning community.

2. Convene a MCLE learning community of six to twelve church teams for an eight-month period.

3. Support your church's participation in the MCLE with regular communication.

4. Provide host arrangements and worship during the session dates:

Session 1— "Getting Started on the Future" _____
DATE

■ Technology session #1 (one hour) _____
DATE

■ Technology session #2 (one hour) _____
DATE

Session 2—"Building Healthy,
Repeatable Patterns" _____
DATE

■ Technology session #3 (one hour) _____
DATE

■ Technology session #4 (one hour) _____
DATE

Session 3— "Telling God's Story" _____
DATE

[FACILITATOR / ORGANIZATION] agrees to:

1. Provide a trained MCLE facilitator for all sessions.

2. Work with the local coordinator and the Association of Churches (name) to support participating churches between the training events.

3. Share your church's learning experience with other churches, for the good of all.

Covenanting Congregation agrees to:

1. Form a mission team to learn on behalf of the congregation, consisting of the pastor (or appointed leader), three lay leaders, and a young adult (aged 15–29).

2. Provide this agreement, signed by the mission team members, designating their willingness to make an eight-month commitment to the MCLE process.

3. Attend all three in-person sessions and each of the four technology sessions.

4. Complete the four-step process to practice healthy, repeatable patterns for community ministry.

5. Design and implement a small, interactive community involvement to practice missional principles, using the results of the four-step process and investing appropriate church resources.

6. Share what your team learns from this experience with the MCLE learning community and with your association of churches.

_____

Church

_____

Address

_____

City / Town

_____

State / Zip

_____

Pastor or Appointed Leader Name (please print):

_____

Signed

_____

E-mail

_____

Lay Leader Team Member Name (please print):

_____

Signed

_____

E-mail

Lay Leader Team Member Name (please print)

Signed

E-mail

Lay Leader Team Member Name (please print)

Signed

E-mail

Young Adult Team Member Name (please print)

Signed

E-mail

Please return your signed MCLE Application and Covenant to your Coordinator:

Name

E-mail

Addendum B
Missional Church Learning Experience
Learning Agreement

1. Who will be your MCLE coordinator? What is their understanding of the responsibilities expected?

2. How many churches will you recruit for the regional learning community?

■ Six minimum, twelve maximum

■ Does your association of churches want to create multiple learning communities?

3. Select *all* dates for sessions (four months between in-person sessions):

Session 1 _____

       Technology #1 _____
       Technology #2 _____

Session 2 _____

       Technology #3 _____
       Technology #4 _____

Session 3 _____

4. What are the details for hosting the learning community for the three in-person sessions of the MCLE (i.e., dates, time, location, meal, snacks, equipment, people involved, cost, worship)?

5. How will the learning community churches be supported between sessions? (Blog or chat room? Coach calls? Pastors' conference calls? How often? Who?)

6. How will you share your MCLE learning community's experiences and lessons learned within your association of churches?

7. What follow-up plans need to be in place to keep the churches learning once the Missional Church Learning Experience is over?

8. What else?

Missional Church Learning Experience
Request

In Partnership with [ORAGANIZATION NAME]

Name of Association of Churches

_____

Date of request

_____

Name of coordinator

_____

Coordinator ministry position

_____

Contact information for coordinator:
Office (or home) phone

_____

Cell phone

_____

E-mail

_____

Mailing address

_____

_____

Having reviewed the Guidelines for the Missional Church Learning Experience, we would like to participate in the MCLE by forming a learning community.

We are in agreement to:
■ provide a coordinator to work with the MCLE facilitator to implement a Missional Church Learning Experience for our association of churches;

■ form a learning community of mission teams from six to twelve churches, with signed agreements thirty days before Session 1 (Addendum A);

■ host arrangements for the three in-person sessions of the learning community;

■ provide support for learning community church teams between training sessions, with assistance from the MCLE facilitator;

■ share lessons learned with other churches for the good of all; and

■ prepare follow-up opportunities for the learning community.

Please sign and date:

Person requesting

_____
Ministry Position   Date

_____
Coordinator

_____
Ministry Position   Date

_____

Please return by mail or e-mail to your MCLE facilitator:

_____
Name

_____
Address

_____
E-mail address

_____
Phone

Change Game Results

Missional Church Learning Experience
Change Game Results

1960–2010

Future Shock by Alvin Toffler, published in 1970, predicted an accelerating rate of change that would challenge humans' ability to adapt without going crazy. Consider these changes that occurred in just fifty years. *What would you add to the list?*

Science & Technology	
1960	**2010**
No permanently orbiting satellites	Thousands of satellites
No Internet	Worldwide access to the Web
Electric typewriters	PCs, laptops, iPad, computers
-------	controlled by touch screen or
-------	voice
Mail	E-mail, texting, attachments
Paper calendar	PDA
Lick stamps	Self-stick stamps

Records	Digital, downloadable music
Ovens	Microwaves
Aluminum foil, wax paper	Plastics, Styrofoam (creating a global waste problem)
Cameras used film	Digital cameras, phone cameras
Pictures sent to processors	Create your own prints
8 mm film cameras	iPhone digital videos
Landline phone (one per family)	iPhones, text, voicemail, e-mail, webcam (one per person)
Land telescope observatories	Hubble Space Telescope, black holes
Microscopes	Electron microscopes
Atoms	Subatomic particles
-------	Particle accelerators
TV–black/white, 18"-screen	HDTV, web access, flat screen
TV–three channels, all American	Cable, satellite, hundreds of channels, global
Movies in theaters	Netflix, DVR, On Demand
Coal furnaces	Heat pumps
Wood construction	Rebar/concrete, fiberglass, Tyvek
Locks	Security systems (codes, fingerprints, iris reader, face and voice recognition, metal detectors, body scans)
Bulletproof vests from cloth/metal	Bulletproof vests made from Kevlar
Shoelaces	Velcro
Maps	GPS (in car devices, on phones)

Canned food	Microwavable, freeze-dried
Hand-powered kitchen gadgets	Myriad electrical kitchen equipment
Electric and coal power plants	Nuclear, solar, wind power
-------	Nanotechnology
-------	Artificial Intelligence
-------	Robotics
-------	Lasers
-------	Space stations
-------	Space travel in reusable craft
Office buildings	Skyscrapers
-------	Quantum physics, particle physics
Weather forecasting–best guess	Doppler radar, satellites
Inventory tags	Barcodes
-------	Night vision goggles
-------	Infrared sensors
-------	Cloning
-------	New life forms created in the lab

Sports & Entertainment

1960	2010
World Series	Super Bowl
Limited number of sports	Plethora of new sports
Limited number of teams	Plethora of new teams
Limited number of TV games	Multiple 24/7 sports channels

-------	Extreme sports
-------	Instant replay
Sports heroes	Drug use, bad behavior
Moderate pay	Multiple millions in pay
Mostly white, male players	Multiracial and women sports
Simple equipment, simple training	Computer training, high-tech equipment
AM radio	Sirius Satellite Radio
Language carefully controlled	Use of bad language in primetime
Modest dress	Revealing dress
Modest sexuality (twin beds)	Explicit sexuality, including homosexuality
Blockbuster movie: *The Ten Commandments*	Blockbuster movie: *Avatar*
Printed materials–typeset	Printed materials–digital publishing
Books–in libraries, bookstores	Books–digital, e-books, print-on-demand, iPad, Kindle, Nook
Children's games–board games	Children's games–Xbox, PlayStation, Nintendo Wii

Transportation

1960	2010
State highways (2 lanes)	Interstate highways (4+ lanes), Super highways (6+ lanes)
Goods primarily moved by rail	Goods primarily moved by tractor trailers

Passenger airplanes–mainly props	Passenger jets
Airplane travel–uncommon	Airplane travel–common
Cars–one per family	Cars–one per driver
Cars made with steel (heavy)	Cars made with lightweight materials
Cars mechanical	Cars computerized
Cars use leaded gas	Cars use variety of fuels, hybrids
Recreation boats built with wood	Recreation boats built with fiberglass
Steam locomotives predominant	Diesel or electric locomotives predominant
-------	Magnetic levitating trains
RV trailers	Motor homes
-------	Jet Ski
-------	ATVs
-------	Snowmobiles
-------	Skyways
-------	Tollways
-------	Tollways with computerized IDs
-------	Vertical-takeoff jet fighters
-------	Stealth jet planes
-------	Drones (unmanned aircraft)
-------	Hovercraft
-------	Supersonic travel, Concord
-------	Segway

Escalators just introduced	Escalators in common use
Submarines	Nuclear-powered submarines, mini-subs

Medicine & Healthcare	
1960	**2010**
Penicillin	Plethora of antibiotics
X-rays	CAT scans, MRIs
-------	Defibrillators
-------	HMOs, specialists
Family doctor	Laser and robotic surgery
Surgery	Surgical glue
Sutures	Dialysis
-------	Transplants
-------	Stem cells used to grow organ replacement
Heart attacks – no treatment	Stop heart attacks while happening, cardiac catheterization, inserting stints
Cancer – surgery, radiation	Cancer – chemotherapy, radiation, surgery, options
Prosthesis – primitive	Prosthesis – robotic, controlled by the brain
Wheelchair – manual	Wheelchairs – motorized, controlled by the brain

Birth control–abstinence, rhythm	Birth control–pill, IUDs, other options
ED–not discussed, no treatment	ED–discussed openly, treated with a pill
Depression–talk therapy, shock therapy	Depression–treated with a pill
Glasses	Contacts, laser surgery
Cosmetic surgery–used little	Cosmetic surgery– commonly used
Infertility–adopt	*In vitro* fertilization, surrogate mothers, international adoptions
Heredity problems– no solutions	DNA mapping, Epinome, gene therapy
Healthcare–non-profit	Healthcare–for profit
Dying assistance–family	Dying assistance–hospice
Euthanasia–not discussed	Euthanasia–a protected right
Insurance–not expensive	Insurance–out-of-control costs
Polio vaccine	Vaccines for many afflictions, even the flu
STD	AIDS

U.S. Culture

1960	2010
Main Street for shopping	Shopping centers, malls, big-box stores

Dress and suit required	Casual–everywhere
Segregation	Civil Rights
Women mainly at home	Women work in any role
Patriotism honored	Nationalism disapproved
Mail by postal carrier	E-mail, texting, fax, social networking websites
Drug use–uncommon	Drug use–common
Alcohol consumption–limited	Alcohol consumption–widespread
Meals–mainly eaten at home with family	Fast food
Family–defined as parents/children	Family–defined as an affinity group
Gang activity–uncommon, mainly urban	Gang activity–common in all communities
Schools–safe	Schools–metal detectors
Religion–common, expected	Religion–uncommon, suspect
TV news–believed to be objective	TV news–believed to be slanted
Sex–not discussed	Sex–openly discussed
Mental illness–not discussed	Mental illness–openly discussed
Abortion–not discussed	Abortion–available, common
Children–should be protected	Children–exposed to harsh realities
Violence–uncommon, shunned	Violence–in every setting, even video games

Change–done slowly	Change–constant, erratic
Marriage–for life	Marriage–divorce common
Single–uncommon	Single–common
Single with children–rare	Single with children–common
-------	Homosexual couples adopting children
Children's extracurricular activities–limited	Children's extracurricular activities–competitive and start young
Fans, open windows in summer	Air conditioning (window units, stand-alones)
Population–small towns, farms	Population–suburban, urban
U.S. population size– 130 million	U.S. population size– 300 million
Immigrants–small population	Immigrants–large population
Euro-Americans dominate	Multiracial common
College–special	College–expected
Graduate school–rare	Graduate school–common
American-made–the norm	China-made–the norm
One landline phone per household	One cell phone/iPhone per person
Talk with friends	Text, social networks (Facebook)
Friday night date	Computer dating (eHarmony, Match.com)
Flea markets for bargains	eBay, Craigslist

Long-distance calls–emergency only	Long-distance calls–common
Travel–rare, close to home	Travel–common, global
Vacations–inexpensive, close to home	Vacations–expensive, global
Second vacation homes–rare	Second vacation homes–common
Shipping packages–expensive, rare	Shipping packages–overnight, common
Energy consumption–limited	Energy consumption–massive
Waste management–local	Waste management–global
Public spaces–open	Public spaces–security
Knowledge of the world–limited	Knowledge of the world–increasing
Cloth diapers	Disposable diapers

Missional Church Learning Experience Steps

Missional Church Learning Experience
Step 1—Building Our Mission Team: Discipleship Central

Preparation

■ Gather your MCLE mission team to plan and implement this assignment.

■ Ask someone to read aloud Matthew 28:16-20.

■ Discuss the following in your group:

❑ Verse 17 states, "They (the eleven disciples) worshiped [Jesus]; but some doubted." In what ways do we doubt Jesus today?

❑ How does Jesus' declaration of his authority (v. 18) change our doubts into faith?

❑ List the verbs used in vv. 19-20. What actions are required in making disciples?

❑ Verse 19 instructs us to "[baptize] them in the name of the Father and of the Son and of the Holy Spirit." What are some ways we can fully immerse new disciples into a relationship with the Father, Son, and Holy Spirit?

■ Pray together, asking for God to guide the creation and implementation of this assignment.

Instructions

Have someone read these instructions aloud:

According to the Matthew 28:16-20 passage, the purpose of the church body is to make disciples. Therefore the first step in becoming a missional church is to build mission teams that practice being authentically Christian while engaging with the community.

There are two reasons your mission team needs to practice being Christian with one another. First, ministry is hard work and the members of your team need the support and discipline of the group to grow in their own discipleship. Second, it takes a disciple to make a disciple. As others join your team along the way, they need to experience an authentic Christian community—a place where disciples are formed and nurtured. To quote the apostle Paul, "If I give all I possess to the poor and give over my body to hardship that I may boast, but do not have love, I gain nothing" (1 Corinthians 13:3).

Your first assignment has two parts: (1) develop a simple plan for keeping your mission team Christ-centered throughout the MCLE process, and (2) develop a simple plan for communicating your MCLE team's efforts to your church.

When you attend Session 2 of the MCLE, your group will tell the learning community how your team is being Christian with one another and how you are communicating your team's efforts with your church.

Suggestions for mission team Christian practice

Think back to the closing Covenant ceremony of Session 1 of the MCLE. A covenant was described as "a promise to do what is right because it is right, regardless of another's response." What would you write as a team covenant? You may want to consider the following:

■ How often will the team meet? What day/time? Where? Who will remind the team?

■ What role will prayer play in your team gatherings? How can you build in prayer for one another, your church, the other churches in your MCLE learning community, your MCLE coordinator and facilitator, and the new teammates that will join you along the way?

■ What other discipleship activities would be helpful to the team's development (e.g., reading the Bible together and discussing how it reflects missional values)?

■ What are some ways the team members could support each other throughout the MCLE process?

■ How will you make others feel welcomed into the team and model the Christian life to those who join the team throughout the process?

Suggestions for communicating with your church

■ List some advantages for your church if your MCLE team does a good job of communicating with the church throughout the MCLE process.

■ List some disadvantages for your church if your MCLE team does not communicate well with your church throughout the MCLE process.

■ Brainstorm ways your team could communicate with the church throughout the MCLE process.

■ Pick a couple ideas and make plans to implement; decide who, what, where, when, and how.

Celebration and Reflection

Congratulations—your team has just completed the first assignment. Celebrate your success. Reflect on some ways your team can regularly remind itself to continue practicing these two team-building patterns: practicing being Christian with your teammates, and communicating with your church.

Missional Church Learning Experience
Step 2—Learning to Listen to Our Community

Preparation
- Gather your MCLE mission team to plan and implement this assignment.
- Ask someone to read aloud Luke 10:25-37.
- Discuss the following in your group:

What effects did Jesus expect the gospel of God's kingdom to have on earth?

Did Jesus expect the disciples who followed him to have an effect upon the world? Name some of the disciples' effects. How did they achieve them?

What effect could you as disciples of Jesus have on your world?

- Pray together, asking for God to guide the creation and implementation of this assignment.

Instructions
Have someone read these instructions aloud:

The first priority in becoming a missional church is to know your community. To help you design your community project, you need to have conversations with people outside your church to learn about your community and its needs.

Your first assignment is to talk with people outside the church and hear their thoughts about your community's needs. You decide who, when, where, and how to do this. You have four weeks to complete Step 2.

When you attend Session 2 of the MCLE, your group will share how you engaged people outside the church in conversation, what happened when you did, and what you learned.

The simplest way to have conversation is to ask questions. One way to complete Step 2 is to write one to three questions that you can ask people who do not attend your church about your community's needs. The questions should be simple but require more than a "yes" or "no" answer. Here are some examples: If you could fix one problem in our town, what do you think would make the biggest difference? What are some of the needs in our community? How could churches help our community more? When have you seen a good example of churches being involved in our community?

Think through the following
How?

How will you distribute the questions? How will you record the responses? How will you collect the answers? How will you determine patterns among the answers that can help you pick a community project?

Who?

Who is going to ask these questions—just the members of your mission team, or will you invite others in your church (or outside) to get involved? If you are going to get others involved, how will you do that? Will you go out to ask questions in pairs?

When?

When will you all go out? Will you go out on the same day and at the same time? Or, will you tell people to go anytime they want and return the results by a specific date and place?

Where?

Where will you ask your questions—on the street, door-to-door, or in familiar locations such as schools, neighborhoods, clubs, etc.?

Gathering / Celebrations / Diagnosis

After your answers are collected, set a time for the mission team (and others who are interested) to gather and talk about the experience. What did you learn? What patterns did you notice? What ideas for a community project have you heard or seen?

Missional Church Learning Experience
Step 3—Looking for Potential Mission
Partners in Our Community

Preparation
- Gather your MCLE mission team to plan and implement this assignment.
- Ask someone to read aloud Mark 3:31-35.
- Discuss the following in your group:

Jesus said that "whoever does the will of God" is his brother, sister, and mother (v. 35, NRSV). What is the "will of God"?

Name some activities being done now that could be considered "the will of God."

How does Jesus expect us to relate to those who do God's will?

- Pray together, asking God to show you these agents in your community and how you might become involved in God's mission with them.

Instructions
Have someone read these instructions aloud:

By now your mission team has had conversations with people outside your church and listened to their ideas about what your community needs (Step 2). This next step will help you find out what God is already doing in response to those needs and discover potential partners in God's mission. Knowing who else is working in your community and what they are doing will help you determine your community project. God may be calling you to get involved with actions initiated by others and in the process develop life-giving relationships. You decide who, where, when, and how to find God's partners in your town. You have four weeks to complete Step 3. When you attend Session 2 of the MCLE, your group will share what you discovered about God's missional actions in your town and possible partnerships.

How?

Brainstorm about where to find potential community partners (e.g., newspapers, yellow pages, community bulletin boards, government offices, chamber of commerce, civic clubs, other churches, websites). How will you uncover patterns in the information you gather and connect needs to resources? How will you keep focused on Christ during your investigative work?

Who?

Decide who will explore each source. Are there others in the church (or outside) who can help? Are there any networks you can contact in your community?

When?

Set a deadline for when you want the information gathered. Set a date, time, and place for your mission team (and others who may be interested) to meet again to review the findings.

Gathering / Celebrations / Diagnosis

When your mission team gathers to share results, will you invite others to help you discuss and discern? Talk about your experiences; are there any common themes? Talk about your spiritual reaction to this information; do you see places where your church fits in naturally and would be good at getting involved? Think back on the conversations you had with people in Step 2 about your community's needs. Are there any gaps between what's being done and what people need? Do you sense a call to any of these needs? Time to pray again.

Missional Church Learning Experience
Step 4—Discerning Our Part in God's Mission

Preparation

■ Gather your MCLE mission team to design your community project outline.

■ Ask someone to read aloud Matthew 25:31-46. As you all listen quietly, reflect on a word, phrase, or thought that stands out for you in this passage. Share with each other what captured your attention.

■ Ask someone to read aloud Matthew 25:31-46 again. As you all listen quietly, reflect on what this passage may be saying to your mission team and your church at this time. Share your thoughts with one another.

■ Pray together, asking God to show you what community project would best serve God's purpose both in your community and for your church. Ask God to show you the where, when, and how to fit in with God's will for this community project.

Instructions

Reflect on Step 2—Learning to Listen to Our Community; what community needs or patterns did your conversations with people outside your church show you?

Reflect on Step 3—Looking for Potential Mission Partners in Our Community; where is God at work, and who is already working with God in your community to bring God's "will on earth as it is in heaven"?

Discuss: where do you feel God is calling your mission team to fit in with God's work in your community? Keep in mind:

■ It doesn't have to be big: even a small step toward community involvement will help you learn and prepare for more. Learn as you go—that's discipleship.

■ It's good to work with another group whose call matches yours—even a non-Christian group that holds values that reflect God's kingdom on earth.

■ You can and should involve people in the project who are not part of your church, including people who will be served.

■ If you have several ideas and can't decide, pick one and save the others for later. Any action that blesses your community will add to God's kingdom-building work.

Community Project Outline: Answer the following questions in writing:

1. Name the project. Giving your project a name helps form a clear identity. For example, a project might be named "Backpacks for Back-to-School Basics."

2. What community need does this project address (Step 2)?

3. What ministry partners could help you with this project (Step 3)?

4. What resources do you need?

5. Answer the who, what, where, when, how questions for your community project:

■ Who will be involved? Who will do what?

■ What exactly do you want people to do? What steps need to happen, and in what order?

■ Where will you meet to do your community project?

■ When will each step happen? When will your community project be complete?

■ How will you invite people to get involved? How will you assess what you learned from your project? How will you support your "authentic faith community" during this community project?

■ How will you celebrate when you are finished?

Your mission team will *bring your community project outline to Session 2* in order to share your plan with your learning community.

Bring enough copies to Session 2 for each church mission team in your learning community, and send copies by e-mail to your MCLE facilitator and coordinator.